Lake's debut offers a candid memoir of her experience with neurogenic bladder and a wealth of practical advice about coping with its daily complications.

An invaluable resource for NB sufferers.

—*Kirkus Review*

JoAnne Lake has created a truly important and entirely engaging book. Gratefully, I do not share JoAnne's diagnosis, at least at this point in my life, but was drawn into her book simply because it is SO interesting. Her wisdom, born of challenges and triumphs, runs throughout — wonderfully applicable to life's everyday demands. Long after finishing her book her guidance still pops into my mind. (Who knew?!)

Thank you! Carpe diem!

—Cathy Bromley, Copy Editor

Facing life with an enduring affliction, especially one that carries intimate secrets about indiscreet body functioning, is weaved with a very emotional component. JoAnne tells her story with honesty and transparency, with a generous heart to help others. She addresses the grief experienced from the loss of a normal life, lack of desire by those close to her to understand her condition as a result of their own embarrassment, the shame and isolation, all of which can lead to feelings of hopelessness and depression. This book is a must read for anyone facing these challenges. As you read, JoAnne will become a trusted friend that you will be grateful to have along on your personal journey.

—Phyllis Oswald Rogers, MA, Licensed Mental Health Counselor

Beyond Embarrassment is for everyone who has ever had to face a daunting medical or physical challenge. It is truly inspiring, offering suggestions for managing life's hurdles. I was engaged with JoAnne's story and have no doubt others will be, too.

While I was prepared for the book's medical content, what really made a lasting impression is JoAnne's honest, forthcoming, and will-to-succeed story. None of us wants to end up with a neurogenic bowel and bladder, as JoAnne shares, but few can overcome what could be such a life-halting condition, as she has done. It is within her generous spirit to tell about her experience. Her goal is to help others avoid the show-stopping situations that she had to confront. I particularly like the Knowledge Nuggets and Tip Time. Each highlights points that JoAnne feels would be of particular importance to readers. And, I agree, they are!

I strongly recommend that health-care professionals read this and share with their patients who would benefit from JoAnne's story. It will make for better, more understanding practitioners, and enhance their patients' will to succeed.

—Elaine Plummer, RN, BSN
Always Discreet Ambassador

Beyond Embarrassment

FOREWORD BY LORA PLASKON, MD, MS

reclaiming your life with neurogenic bladder and bowel

Beyond Embarrassment

JoAnne Lake *and* *Biosleuth* Julia Parker

JoAnne Lake

Julia Parker

Beyond Embarrassment

For information about this title or to order other books and/or electronic media, contact the publisher:

Triumph Media Press
PO Box 59262
Renton, WA 98058
TriumphMediaPress.com

Library of Congress Control Number: 2015908628
ISBN Softcover: 978-0-9964305-4-8
eBook: 978-0-9964305-2-4

Printed in The United States of America
Cover and Interior design: 1106 Design

To Our Mothers . . .

The women to whom we owe the very most

Gloria Elaine . . .

My motivation to do better and the source of unconditional love

E. Joan . . .

Always there for me, offering encouragement through every challenge

Table Of Contents

Author's Note

—Note from Author JoAnne Lake

This book is based on my personal experience in dealing with Neurogenic Bladder and Bowel, and my research into various aspects of these conditions. I am not a doctor, however, and this book does not take the place of consultation with physicians and other health-care providers with suitable expertise. No book, including this one, can take the place of advice and treatment from a qualified health-care professional. Before following my example or using any of the information I share in this book, please consult with your health-care providers to make sure that it is right for you.

References in the book to goods and services of third parties and the trademarks associated with them are for informational purposes only. This book does not endorse, and is not sponsored or endorsed by, any doctors, medical facilities, or manufacturers of medicines or medical devices, or any other goods and services.

I have fictionalized the first names of the individuals identified in the book as "Annika" and "Laura." Any similarity between the fictional first names and the names of real people is strictly coincidental.

Foreword

—Lora Plaskon, MD, MS

I never cease to be amazed at the stoicism and grace of my patients, especially in dealing with an intimate, debilitating issue such as Neurogenic Bladder. JoAnne Lake has written the first book of practical advice and support in dealing with the varied ways Neurogenic Bladder can present obstacles in your life and ways you can overcome your symptoms and get back in control.

When our bodily functions we take for granted go awry, such as something as simple as holding and emptying our urinary bladder at will, it can completely alter how we see ourselves in the world — relationships, body image, self-esteem, and personal worth and ambition in life are all impacted. In dealing with a Neurogenic Bladder, there may be some "simple" fixes to enable normal bladder storing and emptying, but the impact on the psyche can be devastating. Reenvisioning yourself living a normal life with a Neurogenic Bladder involves an internal private process that can feel very alienating. JoAnne Lake is your friend in this process, and her book enables you to see yourself as normal again, realizing you are not alone in the process, giving empathy and support to overcome a very intimate health issue.

Neurogenic Bladder has historically been a term used to describe bladders impacted by spinal cord injury or congenital developmental problems where the nerves between the bladder and brain either were injured or never developed normally. Contemporary concepts of Neurogenic Bladder are more inclusive to include any condition that impacts the normal neuro-urologic controls, (i.e., the brain-bottom nerve connections). Normal neuro-urologic control is a two-way street of communication along nerves between the brain, spinal cord, and peripheral nerves to and from the end organ, the bladder.

Persons may be born with or develop a Neurogenic Bladder. Any condition that impacts brain, spinal cord, or peripheral nerves to and from the bladder may result in Neurogenic Bladder symptoms. Some very common health events may lead to Neurogenic Bladder symptoms such as prolonged labor and vaginal delivery, spinal discopathy with nerve compression and sciatica, pelvic surgery, arthritis, or most any type of pelvic inflammation. Some medications can impact the nerves to and from the bladder. Neurogenic Bladder symptoms may be temporary, and normal function may be recovered, but if symptoms persist longer than three to six months, and the neurologic insult is a permanent injury, and the underlying condition cannot be corrected, then Neurogenic Bladder symptoms will likely persist, and some accommodation and long-term treatment and monitoring will be needed. Millions of Americans are impacted by Neurogenic Bladder. The overall public health costs and impact of Neurogenic Bladder are broad and estimated to be in the billions per year.

Caregivers treating and specializing in Neurogenic Bladder may be hard to find. Traditionally, urologists care for persons with Neurogenic Bladders, but the attention to overall pelvic health may vary from provider to provider. Because there is cross-talk in the pelvic nerves, persons with Neurogenic Bladder are likely to also have sexual and bowel symptoms. Complete pelvic health care should include attention not only to optimizing bladder control, but also care for sexual function and regulating bowels. Neurogenic Bladder may also impact kidney function, so routine monitoring of kidney function is an inherent part of caring for anyone with Neurogenic Bladder. Oftentimes, persons with Neurogenic Bladder are their own best advocates, and this book enables you to ask the right questions and advocate for your overall health.

Dr. Lora Plaskon is a founding member of Athena Women's Health, Issaquah, Washington, and came to her avocation in the spirit of developing a unique place for women's pelvic health care. Her midwestern candor, intuition, and clinical acumen have enabled Dr. Plaskon to be an astute caregiver for women's most intimate pelvic health issues. She is dedicated to the ongoing evolution of improving women's health-care in research and advocacy at a national level through her work with the American Urogynecologic Association and American Urology Association. Dr. Plaskon is an engineer, surgeon, epidemiologist, mother, wife, dog-lover, and avid hiker and explorer of the Pacific Northwest wilds.

Part 1

My Story

1. Diagnosis: Neurogenic Bladder

"We are all faced with a series of great opportunities –
Brilliantly disguised as insoluble problems."

—John Gardner

That Monday, I came to work full of trepidation. I had become exasperated over the weekend as I fumbled and said words that I should not have said, all because I had spent long hours in my home bathroom learning to use a woman's intermittent catheter. I cried several times out of the sheer frustration. My new toileting routine took so long. I felt like I had been given a life sentence to a porcelain throne.

Today would be my first day to use a catheter at work. I had only minutes to find a private place and wash my hands; only then could I struggle to unwrap the lubricant, unwrap the catheter, and then finally find the small orifice on my body to insert it. Thinking about finding that spot on my body made me sweat, though the day was cold.

Walking through the halls of the high school that day, I felt like a freak. I chastised myself for drinking the extra cup of coffee at daybreak. There was little time to catch my breath let alone use the restroom, even on a good day. Worrying about how I would manage emptying my bladder within a fifteen-minute time frame was not what I wanted to think about as I started my day.

Location was the key. I ruled out my initial idea of the nurse's room, even though it had a larger area and a private sink. I worried about the long line of staff and students that might form while I took such a long time. What if someone got sick and needed the bathroom? No, I would use a quiet, private restroom upstairs. The door was usually locked, so it would be perfect.

At the start of my break, I sprinted up the stairs, and, at the top of the flight, I ran into a friend, just starting her break as well. The unending conversation continued. I wanted to lose her and take care of business. It was clear that the discourse was not going to stop, despite the fact that I gave her little encouragement. She followed me to the door and watched fascinated as I unlocked that coveted vacant restroom. I was stunned as she lightly said, "What a good idea to use this rest-room. I'll go after you." What could I say other than, "No, please, go first."

Disgraced, I slipped back into the classroom tardy. After that, I decided to use the nurse's room. I had to stop worrying about creating a long line. I had significant burdens, and getting my time in the toilet had to take precedence. Eventually my technique did improve. I was so grateful for that!

I still do not know why my body betrayed me or the exact chain of events that led to my development of a Neurogenic Bladder, but I did know that things simply were not right anymore. Depression and lethargy filled my life as I tried my best to ignore and push past the feelings of guilt that I experienced because I thought I was just being lazy. Don't get me wrong. I tried my best not to succumb. I lived my life, but, at times, it was especially difficult.

My body felt bloated and full, and my muscles hurt all over. I had pain on my right side that did not go away. Food just did not taste good, and I was frequently tired. My mind would play tricks on me. I had a great family and life, but there was an ever-present heavy feeling – an undercurrent of bad feelings that tainted my activities. There were physical changes that I never expected or ever would have wanted.

My urine flow was so weak that I had to lean forward and press out my urine to void. Gone were the days when I could pee like a racehorse. It all happened so gradually that I did not notice that my condition was worsening year by year.

My bowel would go rogue when I was out on walks. I had repeated accidents and did not understand why. Then my body would do an about-face, and I would go from a state of uncontrollable diarrhea to constipation. Because of the constipation, I developed severe hemorrhoids that caused bleeding and other discomforts. There never seemed to be a balance.

For years, I kept all of these symptoms to myself because of the shame and embarrassment of discussing them with anyone, including my doctor. My days were filled with anxiety, embarrassment, and fear as I tried to manage my condition without understanding why my body was misbehaving in such a humiliating way.

I did try to find out why the pain on the side of my abdomen did not go away. I saw two doctors over a period of years, and both diagnosed me with Irritable Bowel Syndrome, a condition for which I was offered antidepressants, stool softeners, and any number of cures – all to no avail. My symptoms of a pain at the side of my stomach and being chronically tired continued, and I gave up trying to explain what was going on. I tried the antidepressant for a while but stopped because it made me feel like I was in a tunnel. I felt spacey and like I wasn't really part of what was going on around me. So, the pain continued, and I learned to live with it. I knew that I was not well, but I coped primarily by ignoring my many symptoms.

Time for a Change

One morning I woke up just tired of being tired. I was fifty-five years old, my kids were grown, and I had had enough. I was miserable. My body hurt. I ached all over. My pain index went from a slight, constant twinge in my abdomen to screaming discomfort. That morning, a sudden realization came over me. I had to ask myself, "Am I going to die of this?"

It was near the end of the year, so I made a New Year's resolution that I would get to the bottom of why I had lost my zest for life. After years of pain and discomfort, I had to stop pretending that I was just fine and discover why I hurt so much. Dealing with my health issues became paramount.

I still do not understand how I allowed myself to live with such discomfort and tried to ignore it for so many years. I grew up with a mother who would just push past pain and never talk about it. I suppose I am a bit like her. Perhaps I hoped that the pain would go away on its own or that, if I could ignore it, then it was not really serious. However, on that day, overlooking the situation was no longer an option. I changed doctors. I was getting sicker by the day, and I wanted to find out why.

On my first visit, my new family-practice physician ordered a urinalysis. My urine looked unhealthy. It contained leukocytes and red blood cells, telltale signs of trouble. She gave me a slip to get an ultrasound and immediately referred me to a urologist.

At my first urology appointment, I was asked to empty my bladder on my own, and then, as I lay on the examining table, the doctor used a catheter to drain the remaining urine from my bladder. The urine filled a container that held roughly half a gallon. By contrast, most people feel the need to urinate when their bladders contain about two cups of urine. It was evident that my bladder was retaining urine. The urologist told me very little about his findings or what he thought about my condition, perhaps because of time, and asked me to come back the next day to discuss my situation.

I learned that my body had hit a wall. I could not go on like this. Although my bladder and ureters (the tubes that run between the kidneys and bladder) were still relatively healthy, they were being stretched from holding all that urine. I began to understand why my vitality was fleeting. My body was contending with an oversized bladder, and, because I was not completely emptying my bladder of urine, I was living with a bladder infection.

At first, I very much liked my urologist (whom I will refer to as "my first urologist"). He was respectful and kind as he gave me the information about how to treat my condition. At the time, he used terms like flaccid bladder and Neurogenic Bladder, which I had never heard of before. He said I would need to use a woman's intermittent catheter to stay healthy, and then he left to have his nurse explain what this involved.

The urological nurse came in with a red, rubber, size-14 French catheter and had me sit at the end of the examining table. For perspective, a size-14 French catheter tube is only about 0.19 inches, or 4.7 mm, in diameter. The female one we used was six inches long. The nurse had a mirror, and with me sitting on the edge of the examination table, legs spread apart, she showed me the clitoris, my urethral opening, and my vaginal opening. She then had me watch with the mirror as she inserted the catheter into my urethral opening. Next, I tried to insert the catheter with her hand directing mine. We were successful. She told me to do the same thing at home while sitting on the toilet and sent me on my way with five samples and a prescription for catheters.

I can't begin to tell you how difficult that day was. After leaving the doctor's office, I went to buy more catheters. I naively thought I could just run to the drugstore with my prescription and buy what I needed. Wrong! I went to several drugstores before I learned that this product had to be purchased online. Finally, I found a drug store that gave me the number of an online supplier I could call, but I did not understand that I not only had to find a place that sold catheters but also a preferred provider, so my insurance would cover the cost. Eventually, I sorted it out with the help of a sales rep in a local drug store. Luckily, the first online supplier I called was a preferred provider for my insurance company.

Tip Time:

Our bodies change over the years and may never go back to the way they were in our youth. I was shocked by my diagnosis and struggled with the predictable grieving process. Eventually I stopped resisting reality and wrapped my mind around what became my new normal. I realized I had to accept the body I live in today and make the best of it. It made little sense for me to pine away for what was. I had to work with my body, not against it. Did I have a choice? Not unless I was willing to go on as I had before, struggling against the inevitable. I know I feel better accepting my new normal and not begrudging my reality!

When I got home, things did not go well with the catheter. I cried in pain and frustration because it was so hard to find that little spot where I needed to insert it. On reflection, I realized that, while sitting on the toilet, my feet were resting on the floor, creating an angle to the urethral opening that was completely different from what I'd experienced while sitting on the edge of the doctor's exam table, with my feet dangling in open space. It took me so long to complete the process that I felt I was destined to spend the rest of my existence in the bathroom. With practice, I found that, as I relaxed, the whole process became easier.

Soon using a catheter became second nature to me. I settled into a routine. Over the first few months, I had several bladder infections due to using a catheter to aid urination four to six times a day – perhaps using it incorrectly or, more likely, because it was a foreign object put into my urethra and bladder. My urologist prescribed an antibiotic, which I was not willing to take because it was from the fluoroquinolone family and had been shown to lead to severe muscle and joint problems in rare cases. My body had enough problems, and I was not willing to risk having painful cartilage issues along with all the other things going on. My doctor was quite offended when I would not take his drug of choice, and he refused to offer an alternative. He did not tell me why.

Even before this particular event, I had suspected that I needed better care. My first urologist seemed to think that it was acceptable to let me endure painful bladder infections, with cloudy urine. He was very concerned about the overuse of antibiotics, and he told me that bladder infections were normal for me since I used a catheter. He said that it was useless to test my urine for bacteria because my urine would be tainted by a foreign object (the catheter). He instructed me to take Pyridium, a medication that turned my urine orange, to help control the painful bladder. That medication did indeed help with my bladder pain, but, subsequently, the bladder infection continued. I felt afraid and unheard. My body was moving down a path that only nightmares were made of. My urologist insisted on prescribing an antibiotic, again with possible side effects that caused me concern. When he refused to take my objections seriously, I knew I needed to at least explore other options and find a new urologist.

In desperation, I called Dr. Earl Bardin, a urologist I have known since college, during his office hours. I shed many tears during that conversation because I was suffering from a very painful bladder infection, and I felt like a Mac truck had slammed into my abdomen. I explained to him how totally frustrated I was by my doctor's cold response. I really did need help.

He suggested that I try to explore the *why,* the cause of my Neurogenic Bladder. He was concerned about my health, explaining that a Neurogenic Bladder can be a symptom of any number of other health issues. He recommended that I find a neurologist to help find much-needed answers regarding the cause of my Neurogenic Bladder. I valued his advice and was surprised that my first urologist had not already suggested testing to find the cause of my symptoms.

I did three things after I hung up with Earl and stopped crying: I cancelled my next appointment with the first urologist, I made an appointment with a new urologist Earl suggested, and I made an appointment with a neurologist. I just picked out a name from a list. I was lucky, because, as it turned out, he was a good choice. By following through on these three steps, I felt empowered and ready to take control of my life.

Dr. Earl Bardin wrote a prescription to help me take care of that very painful bladder infection, as well. I will forever be thankful to him for his help and friendship on that day when I rather hysterically took him away from his scheduled patients.

Seizing Control

The very next day, I met with the doctor Earl recommended, and I have remained with her to this day. From my first step into that office, I could feel a huge difference. It was decorated beautifully. The sophistication of the décor and feel of the office was warm and inviting – not anything at all like my first urologist's antiseptic, cookie-cutter waiting room. I felt good just walking in the door.

When I met her, I was immediately struck by her earnest and caring attention to what I had to say. During that first appointment, she spent time getting to know not only my condition but also me as a person.

One of my primary objectives in selecting a new urologist was finding a doctor who would listen to my concerns and be a collaborative team member. I want to have a voice in my health-care decisions. I want my doctor to give me sound advice and then work with me, taking into account my concerns, and understand that I have to live with the consequences of all the procedures and medications. I want to adopt a team approach with my health, not a dictatorship.

I was thrilled that my new doctor was willing to work with me on antibiotics. She did not seem offended at all with my many concerns and patiently answered my questions. She looked earnestly in my eyes and showed interest in what I was saying. I liked her from the get-go.

Tip Time:

Don't ignore physical signs; do something.

You can only get help if you ask.

Change can be good!

She did not want to settle for not knowing the cause of my flaccid bladder, the medical term describing my bladder's inability to void normally. She ordered more tests, including urodynamic testing.

First, she addressed a practical approach to bladder infections, an ongoing concern for me. She has a very safe and convenient system for her patients who are susceptible to frequent bladder infections. She gave me a kit with urine-collection cups, lab slips, and a prescription. If I find myself with a bladder infection during a weekend or anytime when she is out of the office, I'm covered. Her only stipulation is that, prior to getting an antibiotic, even in a desperate emergency, I take a urine sample to the lab so a culture can be done. Without taking a culture, it is impossible to find what antibiotic would be most effective. If I am in a great deal of pain, she allows me to start the antibiotic on the prescription in the kit right *after* I take the culture in. With that protocol, there have been times that I later needed to switch to another antibiotic because the culture revealed that I was fighting two types of bugs, or that the antibiotic I started was not as effective against the particular bacteria I was fighting as another one would be. It was clear that she trusted me to do the right thing. Her confidence was empowering.

There was a great deal of discrepancy between the two urologists with regard to the treatment of bladder infections when the office was closed. With my first urologist, if I had a bladder infection on a weekend, I called the doctor on call for help. He said that he did not consider a bladder infection an emergency, to which I thought, *Well, clearly, he's never had one.* He told me to call Urgent Care. I wanted to ask him flippantly if Urgent Care had my medical chart, but I did not. I was very disturbed by this because I am married to a health-care professional, and Randy would always take care of his patients of record, whatever it took and regardless of the day of the week. Either way, I think it is very acceptable to gather the information from the urologist you are seeing to find out how he or she supports their patients when they need help on their days off.

On another visit to my new urological office, I had an appointment with her urological nurse, who helped patients better understand the menagerie of catheters on the market. This was such a change from the first urologist — who simply gave me a prescription for catheters and sent me on my way.

I told the nurse that I was interested in changing to a disposable catheter because I had seen a television advertisement featuring some prelubricated catheters that were very compact. They sounded easier to use. Having a prelubricated catheter would also eliminate the extra step of lubricating the catheter myself.

The nurse knew a medical-supply company I could work with that was already approved by my insurance and carried the type of catheter I was interested in. This saved me hours of frustration trying to match the product with a vendor approved by my insurance plan. She showed me different types of catheters and even gave me samples to try.

At the end of the appointment, I filled out a form and learned that a month's worth of supplies would be mailed to me. The helpfulness of the staff made me feel like I was at a fine hotel, consulting an expert concierge who gives detailed directions and explicit road maps. I was so relieved and completely blessed to go into a new office and have someone who was willing to walk me through that maze.

Two days later, I returned for my urodynamic testing. Electrodes were placed in various locations on my body, with monitors to read how my muscles and nerves reacted when I urinated. I sat on the edge of a chair that lifted up high so my you-know-what was eye level with the woman doing the test. A tube was inserted into my urethra, and water was pumped into my bladder until it felt full. When that happened, I was able to void. After that, I was cathed, so the total amount of water remaining in my bladder could be measured. Then I went in to talk to the doctor about the results.

The test showed the urologist that my ureters and bladder were working perfectly but did not have a connection to my spinal column and perhaps my brain. She explained it looked like I had a spinal cord injury. This was no surprise to me, since, over the years, I had had back issues.

My other appointment was with a neurologist who practiced at a nearby hospital. I needed to figure out *why* I had a Neurogenic Bladder in the first place, and a neurologist was best equipped to do that. I had to wait a few weeks to get in for my first neurology appointment. When I filled out the paperwork, I requested that the test results go to my family-practice doctor and my urologist if the

Tip Time:

Often the best and most helpful people in a physician's office are the receptionists, the schedulers, and the office coordinator. Be sure to get to know them, too.

Questions to ask when selecting a urologist:

- *How are bladder infections treated? Is there a protocol to take care of pain and discomfort over the weekends and holidays?*
- *Is there an expert in the office who can help me locate and learn about the catheters and/or other devices needed to manage my condition?*
- *Will the doctor take the time to make sure I understand the current tests, procedures and medications that can help me?*
- *Is the office clean and in good repair?*

results might indicate the cause of my Neurogenic Bladder. The urologist was running tests, such as the urodynamic testing, that indicated to her how my bladder was functioning. The trip to the neurologist would study the other parts of my body involved in the mechanics of urination: my brain and spinal column.

My first appointment went well. The staff was friendly, and the neurologist was willing to do what it took to understand why I had a Neurogenic Bladder. He told me that, while many tests could be done, his plan was to take it slow and do one test at a time. If the results came back negative, he would order the next test.

As time progressed, I came to realize the value of new medical research in finding the underlying cause of my "medical mystery." I also felt I was tremendously lucky to have a doctor that was so thorough. From the first appointment, he kept impeccable notes and has always followed through in obtaining past medical records and actually reviewing them.

One of the first tests he ordered was an MRI of my brain to look for white spots. A lot of white spots are an indication of Multiple Sclerosis. The development of a few white spots is part of normal aging. I had a few that were consistent with my age; my results were within normal expectations.

I'd had back surgery for a herniated disc in my late forties, so, next, the neurologist wanted to see if my back was contributing to my bladder issues. I had an MRI done on my lower back. The surgical sites looked normal, and the doctor concluded that my back injury and surgery had not influenced my problem.

After those tests came back with no red flags, I had another MRI done on my lower abdomen. It left me a bit nauseous the next day, but the results were favorable, noting nothing wrong. The final test the neurologist ordered was a spinal tap to rule out the possibility of either cancer or Multiple Sclerosis. It took a while to get my results, but I did get good news: no cancer. The Multiple Sclerosis tests were inconclusive.

After a long discussion, the neurologist suggested that I might have Multiple Sclerosis. He told me that 30 percent of people with MS have a Neurogenic Bladder. I was overwhelmed. I began to imagine life with my active family and being left behind because I could not keep up. While there was no clear answer about whether I had Multiple Sclerosis, time would make my diagnosis clear. I needed to be patient and not overthink a situation that I could not do anything about. My mantra has always been to live this life to the fullest every day. I told myself that this was an important time to keep my positive outlook. I was also a little overwhelmed because the two doctors had different ideas as to the cause of my flaccid bladder. My urologist thought it was because of my back, and now my neurologist thought I might have Multiple Sclerosis.

Lottie, a friend of mine, has Multiple Sclerosis. She continues to be a source of inspiration to me as she weaves through her days, making the fabric of her life. When I was told that there was a chance I could have MS, I wanted to ask a most intimate question: did she have a Neurogenic Bladder as well?

We had never discussed this subject before. From our previous conversations, I understood that she went from being a high school sports star to, by her late twenties, feeling like it was taking her muscles forever to recover from after-workout soreness. She became depressed and lethargic because she was chronically tired. Eventually, she was diagnosed with Multiple Sclerosis. She is under a doctor's care and coping the best she can. She avoids getting overheated and no longer tries to exercise for a muscle burn. Instead she enjoys walking and rests as needed.

When I asked Lottie about Neurogenic Bladder, she readily told me that she had difficulty voiding as well. Lottie was the first person I had talked to regarding this very personal topic. Our first conversation about the condition was quite liberating for me, because, in the past, I had always thought of toileting conversations as crude and crass. It was a topic at best avoided, but now I had a reason to discuss this very personal issue with someone who was dealing with exactly the same thing.

Although I still didn't know for certain what had caused my Neurogenic Bladder, I was finally beginning to understand my mystifying symptoms and why my body was acting the way it was. Discovering how this could have happened to me became my top priority.

I also wanted to discover why I had such negative attitudes toward bowel and bladder dysfunction. I tried to dig deep into my past to determine what clues or medical situations may have caused such havoc. Were my childhood experiences the culprits? Why did I feel a pit in my stomach when the doctor told me I had a Neurogenic Bladder? Why did I feel such shame – such horror and shock at the diagnosis that I would now live with a medical condition that involved my bladder. I wished it were another part of my body, so that I would not have to fear I would be the butt of jokes. No one likes to be laughed at.

2. Attitude Check – How Did This Happen to Me?

You can kiss your family and friends good-bye and put miles between you, but, at the same time, you carry them with you in your heart, your mind, your stomach, because you do not just live in a world, but a world lives in you.

—Frederick Buechner[1]

I grew up in Prunedale, a rural area outside of Salinas, California. While I did not get into trouble and was good at flying under the radar, I unfortunately followed the crowd. I can still remember the names of several kids at school who wet their pants or came to school smelling like poop. I feel so guilty about the way the rest of us talked about them behind their backs. Looking back, I am ashamed of taking part in that humiliation. The stigma of these students' accidents and embarrassment followed them throughout their school years, and my involvement in their humiliation no doubt contributed to my own horror and shame when I first realized I was living with a chronic bladder and a bowel condition. Now I knew how they must have felt.

Today, I find myself in many of the same mortifying situations, and I think of the compassion that I did not lend to those classmates. There's nothing I can do for them now other than apologize and try to pay it forward. If you were ridiculed as a child because of incontinence, please hear me say that I am so sorry.

Because of the pain I caused others, I feel it's even more important for me to do my part to help people understand incontinence and bowel issues. I shudder to think of my life now if I had to deal with the catty statements and snickering in which I'd participated as a girl. The kindness of people and the mercy they extend to me today makes all the difference in my life. It gives me courage to get out and the willingness to go forward and not drown in self-pity.

So, the question that continued to plague me was "How did I develop Neurogenic Bladder?" A number of factors might have contributed to my condition. If you have a Neurogenic Bladder, you may find you share some of them. I began to speculate that the activities I took part in during my younger years might have been a factor. For one, I was hard on my spinal column during my youth. We lived on a farm and had to wake up early to feed the animals. Hauling a heavy bale of hay, I used to hurriedly open it up with hay hooks because, as soon as the animals were fed, I could eat breakfast. As a little kid, I would try to lift a saddle up onto a horse's withers and cinch the girth strap by putting my back to the horse and leaning forward as my backside pressed against him, the girth strap over my shoulder. There was always something heavy to lift, and I was too impatient to wait for a parent or other adult to do it for me. I do not remember telling myself to bend at the knees and gave little concern to my body or the consequences of its abuse. I ended up with a really sore back at times, and I remember many hot baths to soothe my young, aching body.

When I started high school, the school bus came all the way out to Prunedale to pick up the farm kids and pack us back to Salinas. I rubbed elbows with town kids, and my world opened up. No more cowgirl dust for me. I dropped out of 4-H and joined swim team, flag girls, and ASB, the student government organization. Besides my $1.35-an-hour job at Fosters Freeze, I had the opportunity to volunteer for a local physical therapist. I helped her with various therapies to enable children with cerebral palsy to go through crawling motions on a table. The hope was that eventually these children would learn to walk on their own.

The therapist and I also made several visits to Camp Harmon, an Easter Seal Camp near Santa Cruz, so she could check on her clients. Those outings opened my eyes to a world of working with children with special needs. I also worked with autistic kids through a physical education class at Alisal High School. My high school years were full of opportunities and books (I specifically recall reading *Christy* by Catherine Marshall) that gave me a desire to work with kids as an adult.

After graduation, I headed to Washington State University (WSU) because my parents had gone there and had often told me wonderful stories about their college days. WSU did not disappoint.

The summer after my sophomore year, I worked at Camp Easter Seal. I had dreamed of being a camp counselor there since my high school days, and I spent a blissful summer by a pool, playing with great kids at Camp Harmon Easter Seal Camp. Some of the campers by birth or accident had lost bladder and bowel control. It was my first introduction to people who were living a fun and full life with that medical condition. They inspired me. Before I met those kids, I had assumed one of the most basic rights of a human being was to use the toilet the way I did every day of my life. That summer I learned differently.

Several kids who came through camp had birth defects such as Spina Bifida or Tethered Cord Syndrome. At first, I did not understand why they were participating in an Easter Seal camp, because they looked like perfectly healthy children. It was only after getting to know them that I realized they had either diapers or wore sacks to collect their urine. After a rough-and-rowdy sword fight with sticks, they stopped to take care of their toileting needs. For them, it was no problem. They knew what to do, so they could return to the next fun camp activity.

Those kids were my first teachers and guides to living a good life and having a positive attitude while dealing with bladder and bowel dysfunction. When I think back to that warm, lovely place under the pungent Bay Trees, I am thankful for their positive input in my life. Their laughs were sweet, and hearing their play at camp that summer showed me the positive perspective we can have amid personal challenges.

The summer after I worked at Camp Harmon, I met my soul mate, Randy. We first connected in a study-abroad program in London. He was from the University of Washington, WSU's rival. We met before the first classes began and made plans to go to Portobello Road, the very famous and extremely large flea market, with a group of classmates the next day. Since I enjoy antiques so much, I was rather slow moving along, but, for some reason, Randy was, too. He told me that he really liked antiques. We laugh about this today because he could not care less about antiques; he cared about me. He still cares about and for me. He is so supportive, and I count myself so blessed throughout all the phases of life we have experienced together.

We were married several weeks after I graduated from college after his first year of dental school. The dental school years were full of adventure. I worked two jobs while completing a fifth year at Seattle

University. We enjoyed a lot of hiking and, only if you have hiked the trails of the Hoh River Valley, Lake Ozette, or Mt. Rainier, will you understand what drove us to the Washington wilderness during those busy years.

We had our trials, too, because I had three miscarriages, two early and one late, a stillborn little boy. We shared deep moments of grief together, which only drew us closer. We were wonderfully in love and felt hopeful about our future.

We were filled with wanderlust. After Randy graduated from dental school, we traveled to Chichicastenango, Guatemala, for a summer to work at a dental clinic. We came home to Seattle, and that fall we left for Kitzingen, Germany. Randy had joined the Army Dental Corps, and Kitzingen was his first duty station. I was almost six months pregnant, the same point in my pregnancy I had been when we lost our first son. We were so excited to move to Germany and see Europe again. I did not think my pregnancy was an issue, even with my history of miscarriages; we felt that God would take care of us.

Vaginal Delivery

Three months later, at the age of twenty-six, I gave birth to my first child. During my pregnancy, the doctors missed some health issues. They realized I had gestational diabetes only days before my daughter was born. I was surprised to learn this because routine urinalysis should have caught the problem much earlier. I had been leaving urine specimens at every doctor visit during the last months of pregnancy. If I had it to do over again, I would be more proactive. I would ask why each test was recommended and follow up on each test result. A lesson learned.

I delivered a ten-pound baby. Not only was she large, but she was in a transverse position. After I pushed for quite a while, the doctors made a last-ditch effort to assist labor with forceps. The forceps cut into my birth canal, and I lost a lot of blood.

I do not remember much after that delivery. I was later told that the doctors spent a great deal of time stitching me up. When my beautiful child was finally brought to me, I could not lift my arms to hold her. I thought the doctors had given me a powerful drug. They had not. The amount of blood I had lost because of the forceps laceration had left me that weak. Once I had a blood transfusion, my energy returned, and I could finally experience the joy of holding my child for the first time. It was magic. I could not believe how perfect she was and how her heart-shaped lips were so beautiful.

Knowledge Nugget:

Studies have shown a correlation between difficult vaginal deliveries and subsequent urological problems. Contributing factors can include the age and health of the mother and/or damage to nerves of the pelvic floor. A recent study found "about four-fifths of women with urinary incontinence three months after childbirth still had problems twelve years later,"[2] regardless of efforts to strengthen pelvic muscles with floor exercise.

Only much later did I learn that some women who have difficult vaginal deliveries are later diagnosed with Neurogenic Bladder and Bowel.

Two years after the birth of my daughter, my son joined the scene at the same army hospital. Because he was two pounds lighter, it was an easy delivery. However, during the earlier delivery, no one had detected that I am Rh positive and my daughter is Rh negative, so I was not given a RhoGAM shot to protect my future children. Therefore, my newborn son's liver had to work extra hard to dispel the toxins in his body. He was under the bili lights for a week, with the threat of a blood transfusion hanging over him. He looked so little under the lights, all I wanted to do was take him home. In the end, it all turned out well, but I was told that my childbearing days were over because of Rh-factor complications.

We left Germany and, for a year, enjoyed life at Fort Ord, California, near my family, who still lived in Prunedale. My kids had grandparents, cousins, and a highly popular aunt and uncle nearby with whom they made many joyful memories. We relished riding the horses and playing with all the animals on the farm.

That wonderful year came to an end too fast. My husband, Randy, was invited to join a dental practice in Washington. So we packed up for this last move, settling to raise our family in the outskirts of Seattle. I was in the peak of health, and, as a young family, we enjoyed a robust lifestyle.

We were not done adding to our family, however. Six years after the birth of our son, we adopted a two-year-old boy. Seven years after that, we adopted a nine-year-old girl. Both children are from Colombia. Our family felt complete. All four of my kids excelled in sports, so that was particularly fun for me as a PE teacher. Our family of six was happy and strong, and confident that we could tackle whatever life threw at us because we had each other.

Surgical Trauma

Vaginal Hysterectomy

At the age of forty-three, I had a vaginal hysterectomy, and, at the time, I was glad I did. My periods were lasting longer than three weeks at a time, and the nearly constant loss of blood was making me weak. It was hard keeping my clothes clean and my spirits up. To say I was desperate is an understatement. Now that I look back, I might have acted rashly; I definitely acted without informing myself of the possible consequences.

My family-practice doctor had retired, so I was not seeing a physician on a regular basis. I know now that it is not a good idea to be without anyone overseeing my medical care, especially for an extended time period. I should have started with a new doctor right away. But I had always enjoyed good health and youthfully felt I did not require any routine medical care. Doctor appointments were something I made for my children, not for myself. Now I understand that one of the best things we can do for ourselves is to have consistent, annual well-checks. Perhaps, in my case, things would not have gotten so out of hand if I had.

I decided to try a new obstetrician-gynecologist, for whom I did not seek a personal recommendation. I selected her because her office was near my home. After I described my symptoms, she ordered an ultrasound. The results showed that I had fibroid tumors. She suggested that I have a hysterectomy. I was so ready to be done with the tired feeling and inconvenience that I would have offered up my first-born child in exchange for a solution. A hysterectomy sounded like a piece of cake and would put to an end the issues I was so tired of.

First, I had shots to shrink the tumors. After a few months of injections, I went to the hospital for a vaginal hysterectomy. No need for an abdominal incision: an easy pass through the vagina would do the trick. I was relieved to hear that, because the recuperation time would be minimal. They would go in and remove both my uterus and my cervix. From that point on, there would be no need for pap smears. It all sounded great. Who would have ever thought that I might endure consequences from that for the rest of my life?

Years later, I was reading *A Woman's Guide to Urinary Incontinence*[3], a Johns Hopkins Press Health Book by Rene Genadry, MD, and Jacek L. Mostwin, MD. I learned that the cervix and bladder share some nerves, as well as surrounding muscle and ligament supports. I will never forget these words:

> *"The greatest potential for negative effect on the urinary system after a hysterectomy comes from damage to the nerves which extend toward the bladder, since they are detached when the cervix is removed. When the cervix is removed, it is likely that nerve damage will occur because the ligaments of the pelvic region are cut during the operation. Some women will develop incontinence soon after or several years after the operation."*

Suddenly I realized for the first time that my Neurogenic Bladder and Bowel really could have been caused by my vaginal hysterectomy. I experienced a flood of emotions because the book also mentioned that only in severe circumstances should a woman's cervix be removed as part of

Knowledge Nugget:

Both hard physical work and past gynecological surgeries are risk factors for urinary incontinence (UI)[4]. Major pelvic surgery, including radical hysterectomy, is known to cause bladder dysfunction. In his article "Neurogenic Bladder," Dr. Raymond R. Rackley states that "as many as 80 percent of affected patients will experience spontaneous recovery of function within six months after surgery."[5] That leaves 20 percent or more who will continue to have problems. Feelings of extreme shame and embarrassment that accompany disclosure of UI often lead to inaction or significant delay in seeking help, which could ultimately contribute to additional damage to organs of the urinary tract.

a hysterectomy. Are fibroid tumors extreme? At the time I had the hysterectomy, I had no comprehension of the possible complications that could arise. For years, I experienced stomach aches, as my bladder stretched and stretched. Now I know there is a strong possibility this could be why I have a Neurogenic Bladder – or at least a contributing factor.

I immediately sought to confirm this information from other sources, so I went to the Internet. I found a notable lack of information online to corroborate what I'd learned in the book, at least concerning the removal of my cervix as a possible source of my Neurogenic Bladder. I repeatedly read that the consequence of the removal of a woman's cervix might be a lessened experience of orgasm; no other sources mentioned that major damage to the urinary tract or the basic function of urine elimination could be interrupted as a result of this surgery.

I became increasingly discouraged and even angry as I continued my search. Assuredly, orgasm is important, but a basic Web search provided little information about the possibility that cutting nerves and ligaments at the cervix can lead to Neurogenic Bladder. Why is there so little information available about the connection

Tip Time:

Before you have surgery or any procedure, ask to see the paperwork. Take it home, and read what it says. Consider if eliminating or reducing the symptoms of the condition you're currently enduring are worth the risks. Take the time to find out if there is an alternative treatment. Talk to close family and friends who may have additional information. Never experiment haphazardly with your health; it is a beautiful, yet fragile thing! It is always wise to get a second opinion. Remember—it is your body, and you will live with it the rest of your life.

between the removal of the cervix and subsequent bladder and bowel problems? Apparently there are priorities in the presentation of medical literature, and the Neurogenic Bladder connection isn't one of them.

I realize the medical field is trying to do what is best and is slowly moving forward. Unfortunately we are sometimes guinea pigs for some well-meaning doctors. In my case, I feel like I rushed into the hysterectomy. I should have taken the time to be better informed. It is not always possible, I know, and all we can do is trust the advice of our medical team, who work with the latest accepted-care standards. We need to be aware when we sign those medical waivers that real risks exist with almost any medical procedure, and we need to pay attention to those risks. Over time, as the medical field's understanding of how our bodies work changes, so do "best practices." So no matter how careful we are, we may face unforeseen consequences down the road. Be your own advocate.

It makes me melancholy, though, thinking that perhaps things could be different.

Back Surgery Impact to Spinal Cord

I was not finished with surgery. In my late forties, I had back surgery to correct a herniated disc. An MRI the year before determined that I had two herniated discs and one bulging disc. My back would hurt now and then, but that fateful year, things changed. I experienced an explosion of pain. When my back pain set in, my legs would buckle. It was very frightening. To this day I have no idea why this happened. Perhaps it was the cumulative wear and tear, and stress. My back just seized up and froze. For a week, I had to crawl to get around. I lost all of my normal sense of the urge to urinate. When I did feel the urge, I was unable to reach the toilet in time. I needed to use a bedpan to relieve myself. This was the first time I'd experienced incontinence. After a week or so, I was up and running again, and the incontinence seemed to improve on its own. My biggest lingering symptom was a numb leg and foot. I needed the surgery to fend off "drop foot," a condition of paralysis that would have prevented me from lifting my foot as I walked.

While the surgery helped, I have nerve damage in my lower body. It continues to cause continuous numbness along the shin of my right leg and the top of my foot. Neurogenic Bladder and Bowel are commonly caused by a spinal-cord injury or surgical procedures that cause nerve damage. Either one of these, or both, could be a contributor to my condition. Perhaps my failing back could have caused my Neurogenic Bladder.

Tip Time:

Over our lifetimes, our backs can be strained, leading to progressive, degenerative wear and tear. Remember to always bend at the knees as you lift heavy objects, and treat your back kindly.

Like me, you may find that any number of events and health issues may have contributed to the development of your Neurogenic Bladder. Alternatively, a single event, such as a traumatic spinal injury, may be responsible. It's also important to realize that bowel issues you may be dealing with can be related to your Neurogenic Bladder. It took several years after my diagnosis of Neurogenic Bladder for me to come to understand this aspect of my condition. And it's only as I began reading and asking questions that I began to understand the unique challenges of Neurogenic Bowel.

3. Bowel Journey . . . from Symptoms to Survival

For years, I had a problem with constipation. My stools were very hard, almost like rocks, despite the fact that I usually tried to eat a high-fiber diet and got daily exercise. Every day before work, I took a three-mile walk with my neighbor. To my horror, I sometimes lost control of my bowels by the end of the walk. Beads of sweat would form on my forehead even on cold days as I tried to think of an easy exit route. I stayed on the outskirts, hoping to become invisible, anything to avoid drawing attention to myself, and get away as soon as possible.

> LOL
>
> **Chuckle Time!**
>
> Three engineering students were discussing the possible designers of the human body. One said, "It was a mechanical engineer. Just look at all the joints." Another said, "No, it was an electrical engineer. The nervous system has many thousands of electrical connections."
>
> The last said, "Actually it was a civil engineer. Who else would run a toxic waste pipeline through a recreational area?[1]"

Before I was diagnosed with Neurogenic Bowel, I mentioned my problems with constipation and uncontrolled bowel movements to my family-practice doctor. He told me it was probably due to damage in my back from herniated and bulging disks. He prescribed stool softeners. They helped, but I stopped taking them because I was afraid that I would become dependent on them. I did not understand that my condition was permanent. When my symptoms came back, I was surprised and too embarrassed to raise the subject with him again. Besides the doctor, whom could I ask?

Even after I was diagnosed with Urine Retention and a Neurogenic Bladder, I did not realize that I had a chronically sluggish bowel. Had I been better informed, I might have realized I was suffering from something else "abnormal." Looking back, I wonder why the urologist who made my initial Neurogenic Bladder diagnosis did not ask me about my bowel movements. While not everyone with bladder problems also has bowel issues, many of us do. Even if my urologist had not planned to treat that part of my body, it would have helped me to understand that, when there are bladder problems, bowel problems are very common. I didn't stop to think that these symptoms could in any way be connected to my Neurogenic Bladder. They involved two different, self-contained systems, didn't they?

My bowel issues further complicated my already-challenging life. At times, because of the harsh laxatives I took, I had abdominal cramping punctuated by bouts of severe diarrhea. At other times, I experienced harsh constipation. Either way, my success in getting to the toilet fast was the difference between a good day and a bad one.

The worst part of my bowel problems was having no idea what was triggering the accidents, contributing to the most embarrassing part of my day. I had no control over the situation. I could feel my freedom to live life as I chose being peeled away from me. Who wants to go walking with a friend, knowing that at any moment she could have a foul-smelling accident? I worried and I prayed.

What about work? Now there was a tricky situation, for sure. I was lucky with my job because I had the support of the school nurse. "No problem," our school nurse said. "We have a shower here at school." I have not needed the shower at school, but I always had a change of clothes in my car, just in case. Just knowing it was there helped a lot. Staying at home for the rest of my life was not an option. I had to find a solution.

Knowledge Nugget:

Ulcerative Colitis/Inflammatory bowel disease (IBD) and Inflammatory Bowel Syndrome (IBS) might be confused with Neurogenic Bowel as they also result in abnormal stools or a loss of bowel control. IBD is the result of chronic inflammation of the bowel, however, unlike Neurogenic Bowel which is the result of a loss of neurologic control of the bowel.

I went on like this for another couple of years before I realized from my reading that both my bladder and bowel are influenced by the sacral nerve. I learned that not everyone with Neurogenic Bowel has a damaged sacral nerve, but, since mine is damaged, it could cause problems with both my bladder and bowel functions. The symptoms run in tandem.

Thanks to my reading and discussions with my second urologist and neurologist, I came to better understand my situation. I can now work with it. I can plan. And that puts me in control.

Later I came to understand better why my bowels would move uncontrollably. Stool built up in my colon and had to go somewhere. It was rock hard because, at the time, I did not understand my unique digestive system. Diarrhea happened because I was using harsh laxatives.

These days, my life is much simpler. Food is the key to my comfort, and I need to pay careful attention. Rather than let my stool collect in my gut for a long time, I make it a goal to have a bowel movement every morning. If that happens, I am fairly safe for the day. Eating raw foods helps me with that. I have read that the perfect poop is an S shape, not too hard, not too runny. Speaking for myself and my own situation, being deliberate with my food helps me attain perfection.

Tip Time:

When walking, hiking, or participating in other exercise away from home, prepare so you can avoid these issues:

Emotional Embarrassment: *The risk of ending up with a smelly, mucky mess in a potentially remote area where you cannot easily clean yourself.*

Recommendation: *Bring plastic zip-lock bags, hand sanitizer, and wipes. The trees serve as your toilet stall, and, luckily, the squirrels have promised to keep your secret.*

Risk of Bladder Infection: *The ever-increasing concern of risking yet another bladder infection which will occur if you cannot cleanse your skin thoroughly after a bout of diarrhea. Feces have lots of bacteria, and even a speck can cause a bladder infection a few days later. I thoroughly wash myself with antibacterial soap before I use a catheter to pee.*

Recommendation: *Do not cath yourself until you get back from the hike and have taken a shower using antibacterial soap.*

My heart goes out to people who, for whatever reason, need to be sedentary and do not have the opportunity to include physical activity in their schedules. I know from times when I have been inactive that other measures can be taken to aid the elimination process – for example, the use of bowel irrigation systems such as Peristeen or an enema. For right now, I am thankful that activity and meal planning do the trick for me.

Knowledge Nugget:

Hemorrhoids are large veins in the anus or lower rectum that swell under pressure, such as straining to have a bowel movement. They can also occur during childbirth. They often go unnoticed and usually clear up after a few days, but they can cause long-lasting discomfort and bleeding.

Hemorrhoids

For years I suffered from rock-hard stools. It felt more like I was giving birth to a ten-pound baby than having a bowel movement, due to my Neurogenic Bowel. Big bowel movements moving down and tearing the tissue inside my lower rectum and anus caused the blood vessels in that area to become enlarged and caused intense discomfort and unrelenting itching. After years of laying those eggs, it is no wonder I have the hemorrhoids that I do! This is not an uncommon situation for those of us with Neurogenic Bowel.

Dealing with hemorrhoids is an ongoing battle for me. I try to keep a positive attitude. No giving up a grand lifestyle for me – well, most of the time! As I got ready to step out one summer for a high school reunion, I wanted to buy *the* dress that would wow folks. I wanted to strut out and feel proud, but first I had to get the symptoms from my hemorrhoids under control. Aside from causing bleeding and discomfort, sometimes they just itched like crazy.

Tip Time:

For a looser stool . . .

I eat beans, kiwi, prunes, apple juice, all kinds of raw fruit and vegetables – any food product that has fiber. I also make sure I am drinking plenty of water.

If I get really desperate, I use a tea called Smooth Move. One cup goes a long way, so be careful not to overdo.

My Everyday Practices:

- *I eat at regular times.*
- *I drink plenty of water.*
- *I try to exercise at least by walking.*
- *I take a stool softener only if I really need it.*

Diarrhea aggravates my hemorrhoids the most. For some reason, it causes a searing, burning pain, so I watch my diet and activities to reduce the chances of developing diarrhea. My doctor has prescribed a suppository that helps shrink the inflamed tissue so I don't feel as much discomfort. In the end, I did indeed go shopping with a girlfriend and got that cute dress. I had so much fun at my high school reunion that I did not notice my hemorrhoids. Do not let symptoms get in your way! Manage them and go have a good time!

Live Joyfully Within our Limitations

It would be so easy for me to give up and not even try to go on long hikes, work, or enjoy socializing with large groups of people. Yet life is much more rewarding when I don't allow my physical disabilities to keep me locked up at home, separated from people I care about, and inevitably falling into depression.

As normal as I want my life to be and as hard as I fight to be involved in ordinary activities, I do need to realize that some activities I love are no longer possible. Before my diagnosis, my husband, Randy, and I traveled together on medical-mission trips to Guatemala, Colombia, and Mexico to help people in remote locations. My husband, the dentist, filled and drilled. I tried being his assistant but failed miserably because of my queasy stomach at the sight of blood and spit. If a vision clinic was nearby, I helped by passing out used glasses to grateful recipients. These glasses were donated by the Lion's Club and labeled with the prescription of the lenses, so each pair could be matched up with the person needing them.

> **Tip Time:**
>
> *To help manage itching and avoid discomfort... I carry along moist towelettes. Keeping myself clean helps with itching and general discomfort. Avoid wiping too hard, which can lead to bleeding. Creams and salves can be purchased over-the-counter to reduce itching.*

One time I was a team cook, and I could always help out with the children. Wherever we were, babies needed hugs, and kids needed play times. I was there to help. We had the opportunity to meet such lovely people and were able to share our faith. Our passion for changing lives did not end in the mission field. We even brought our work home, adopting our two youngest children from Colombia.

But access to clean water is difficult-to-impossible in these areas. My husband and I needed to remember to use bottled water just to brush our teeth. It was not always easy to take a daily shower. The purity of the water was questionable, leaving me vulnerable to bladder infections and diarrhea. Without prompt lab tests and appropriate treatment from medical professionals, my urinary tract was at risk for further damage, which could have extended to my kidneys.

These trips were also very strenuous. Coming down with a bladder infection hindered my ability to be a vital member of the team and placed added stress on other team members, who had to take on what I could not do. So, in order to maintain as healthy and normal a life as possible and to avoid knowingly putting others in difficult situations, I must now forego these trips.

But while Neurogenic Bladder and Bowel have changed my routine and eliminated some activities I love, they have not taken my joy away. Through all of this, I am a firm believer that, if God closes a door, he opens up a window. My husband can easily go on short medical-mission trips without me, and I get no pressure from him to do something I am simply unable to do. Recently we volunteered to work at a local building site, pulling weeds and painting. Soon the facility will house single women and their children. Another time, we cooked a meal for a homeless shelter, and, on several occasions, we have served a meal. These projects are so fun, and they give me the opportunity to help others in need without having to travel overnight.

I can usually cope with bowel and bladder issues relatively easily if there is a toilet nearby. But what if I want to test fate? What if I would rather experience a day trekking through the wilderness, looking out over the ocean, collecting sea glass, and enjoying the wonder of the world? Is it worth the risk? *Yes, it is very much worth the risk!*

One summer ritual we plan every year is a nine-mile hike, on the Lake Ozette Trail with friends. Crazy, you say? No, not really, because I plan ahead. My family, my friends, my life matter – not my body's random ways. I share my stories because I like to live and celebrate life. My prayer for you is that, like the Nike ad, you, too, will "Just do it."

4. Bladder Infections: Signs and Solutions

In the day of prosperity be joyful, but in the day of adversity, consider: God also hath set the one over against the other, to the end that man should find nothing after him.

—Eccles.7:14 [Authorized (King James) Version]

I don't mean to whine, but this business of constantly fighting off bladder infections is really a pain. Sometimes it seems as if I barely complete one series of antibiotics before I get another one and need to repeat the treatment. Bladder infections are my most worrisome problem. They hit me when I least expect them and when they are most inconvenient. Here's my diary of a typical bladder infection:

Saturday: Went out with friends. Perhaps I got food poisoning, because I threw up all night and had diarrhea. I am out of state and far from home.

Sunday: Feel the tightness and urgency of a bladder infection, but I'm not worrying about it, because my urine is not cloudy.

Monday: Drank water all day. Symptoms are not improving. I feel like I could punch my fist through the wall.

Tuesday: A major disappointment. I could not wish my fate away. Deep down, I knew I had a bladder infection. Today's cloudy urine confirms it. Take urine sample to the lab so they can determine what bacteria is causing the infection. They tell me it will be twenty-four hours before the preliminary report is ready and another day for the final report.

Wednesday-Thursday: Waiting for lab results. I have a sharp pain in my bladder and ache all over. Food does not taste good, and jokes are not funny at all. I fly back home, hurting all the way, and call my doctor's office to see if the lab results are in. They are not.

Friday: I'm up at 4:30 a.m. because of pain. I have no energy. I need to wait until eight o'clock for the doctor's office to open. I now have a raging bladder infection with cloudy, stinky urine. I call the doctor's office two times to see if they have the test results. They don't even have the preliminary report that should have been done by Wednesday. I call the lab myself and beg them to send the report. (I want them to feel my fierce, explosive, vehement pain so they will hurry up.) I'm heading out of town for a romantic ocean getaway with my husband. I pray, "God, help me. I do not feel so romantic with this bladder infection." Finally at twelve noon, I am in the drugstore, waiting for my relief. What a week!

The Next Week: Have been taking Bactrim for seven days. After the second day, I started experiencing some relief. I need to go out of town soon. I will never leave town again without some emergency antibiotics.

Your experience may be different from mine, but my bladder infections usually follow a hauntingly similar pattern. The day before, I begin to feel tired and have a general sense of discomfort. I feel crabby. Sometimes I fall into despair. I chastise myself for just being so lazy. The next day, my labia start burning, and, at times, my urine smells like ammonia. I have pain in my bladder, and I feel so disappointed because I have been fastidious in my personal hygiene in an attempt to avoid this situation. I go from my normal state of not feeling the urge to urinate to needing to urinate more frequently. On rare occasions, I have wet my pants because I lost the race to the toilet.

I cramp and experience slight or, sometimes, severe bladder pain. I am ready for it to stop! Because my catheter use protects my urethra from direct contact with urine, I do not suffer the painful urination most women feel with a bladder infection. Nevertheless, my bladder tightens up and feels strange, even painful. It might seem logical that the pain would be limited to the pelvic area, but, for many people, myself included, the whole body is in pain.

Besides being extremely uncomfortable, recurring infections take an emotional toll on me. They remind me of my frailty, my weaknesses. I'm usually a cheery, optimistic person, but when I'm having a bladder infection, I become really grumpy with my family and just go through the motions at work. I'm more likely to worry about the long-term implications of my condition. For instance, because I have never been able to recover from a bladder infection without taking antibiotics, I start wondering what I will do if I find myself in a situation where either I don't have ready access to antibiotics or I become resistant to the drugs. My husband shared an article with me that he read about women becoming crazy because of bladder infections. I wonder if he was trying to hint that I need an attitude check when I feel an infection brewing.

So many times the feeling of sheer desperation and gloom has come over me. I am quick to anger, and I feel tense and agitated. I am caught off guard because I don't always recognize that the onset of a bladder infection could be causing my feelings of gloom. Then, the next day, it is evident that I have a bladder infection, and I understand why I was so down the day before. The physical and emotional are so tightly interwoven for me.

Knowledge Nugget:

Bladder infections are a serious consequence of Neurogenic Bladder and its management. The bladder is designed to be a contained environment and is closely linked to the kidneys, which drain into it. Too many infections can lead to damage, scarring, and less-effective kidneys. An untreated Urinary Tract Infection can cause problems outside of the urinary tract. During pregnancy, for instance, a UTI could result in a premature birth or high blood pressure, and they more frequently involve the kidneys.[1]

Realizing that bladder infections are, unfortunately, a way of life for those of us with Neurogenic Bladder, I have developed a two-pronged approach to them with the help of my doctors. Please remember that you should not start doing anything in the following lists unless you have first discussed it with a doctor who is familiar with your situation.

Tip Time:

If your doctor suggests that you ignore a symptom, but in your heart and intellect you really know it just cannot be ignored, either challenge the decision or get a second opinion. Not all doctors are equal, and they are capable of making mistakes.

Prevention

The first key to living with bladder infections is to do everything possible to avoid them. I will get plenty of bladder infections for reasons I can't control, so I do everything I can to eliminate contracting avoidable ones.

Prevention starts with cleanliness. Exposing the urethra to unsanitary conditions, including fecal matter, greatly increases the chance of developing an infection. I shower daily and wash my hands frequently, using antibacterial soap. Before I use a catheter, I wash my hands like a heart surgeon going in to perform surgery, sudsing my hands in soapy water. I never urinate at the same time I'm having a bowel movement for fear of cross-contamination. Sometimes by wiping, you can inadvertently push stool near or into your urethra. After a bowel movement, I use a peri bottle (a plastic bottle that can be filled with water to squirt the perineum, the area around the rectum, to help keep it clean) and shower if it's available. If I had a bidet, I'd use that. Women and girls should always wipe from front to back. These practices of cleanliness will help prevent a bladder infection.

I use bio-identical hormone creams. These are estrogen creams available by prescription that are applied to the inner vaginal labia and are usually given to post-menopausal women. Because I insert a catheter several times a day, this area can become inflamed. Topical estrogen creams keep the labia supple and healthy, preventing the cracked skin that can occur when this area is irritated. Broken skin is an open invitation for infection, so when the tissue is kept healthy, it is better able to resist infection. Bio-identical hormones also can change the pH level of the labia, making it more hostile to the bacteria in that area that can cause infections. Consult your doctor to see if estrogen creams may be helpful for you.

I try to do good things for my body. Infection is easier to prevent if I keep my body in general and my pelvic area in particular as healthy as possible. Antibiotics kill both good and bad bacteria, so I take probiotics to replace the good bacteria in my gut or intestines that have been lost. I drink lots of water, exercise, and eat food that I enjoy that is also good for me. The stronger my body is, the easier it is for it to fight infections when they happen.

My Treatment Protocol

In spite of my best efforts, I do get bladder infections. The origin, or most common cause, is unknown. It could be diarrhea, which is due to a bad bug or the result of dealing with my Neurogenic Bowel. It makes keeping scrupulously clean more difficult. Every time I insert a catheter into my body, I'm running the risk of introducing bad bacteria. Beyond continuing to do the things I find helpful in preventing infections, I also take these steps for treatment.

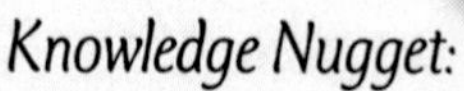

Knowledge Nugget:

Cranberry juice has long been thought to help fight off bladder infections, apparently because a component in cranberries interferes with the attachment of the infection causing bacteria to the cells lining the bladder and urethra. Studies, however, show mixed results, indicating that sometimes cranberry juice helps, and sometimes it doesn't. Because the type of bacteria colonizing the bladder determines how difficult it is to prevent their attachment, women who chronically catheterize are not as likely to respond to the benefits of cranberry juice.[2] Your doctor can determine, through lab analysis, the type of bacteria that is causing your UTI and will know if it is worth trying supplements like cranberry juice.

I take my symptoms seriously. Maybe in part because I don't want to admit I'm having yet another bladder infection, it's tempting to ignore the bladder pain, the cloudy urine, the general malaise. But the sooner an infection is identified and treated, the sooner – and more easily – it will clear up.

I get labs done to confirm that I have a bladder infection and determine which bacteria are causing it. I get a urine specimen to the lab whenever I feel a bladder infection coming on. (This is the one time I don't drink lots of water. It can dilute the urine specimen and create unreliable results.) If my urine is cloudy, I am very suspicious because cloudy urine is a surefire indication of infection for me. I try to wait until the test is completed before taking any medication, but sometimes, when I am suffering with a great deal of pain, I use the emergency antibiotic my doctor has prescribed for me. It will offer some relief.

I consult with my doctor or staff member, whom I trust. Because I have a chronic condition, I need to have a doctor in whom I have confidence. My health and well-being can literally depend on our ability to communicate clearly with one another about critical and personal issues. Neurogenic Bladder and the frequent bladder infections it can produce are not to be treated through the lottery system of an Urgent Care center. Nor are they best treated by a doctor I can't relate to well or whom I don't trust.

I still get mad when I think about my first urologist. He believed that, because I cath, there was no point in lab tests since foreign bacteria would always be in my urine. He told me to "white-knuckle" through my frequent infections. He said cloudy, stinky urine was fine. It was part of my condition. After I changed urologists and I had my urine tested for the first time, the lab tests revealed I had a chronic staph infection that was causing repeated bladder infections. A twenty-day regimen of low-dose antibiotics cleared up the staph infection. I wonder what would have happened if I had continued going to a doctor who refused to do the testing needed to determine what kind of infection I had. I feel fortunate that I was able to find a doctor who listens to me and is not satisfied with accepting the status quo. She has earned my trust.

Whether I receive good or bad medical care, medical tests being the same, the monetary cost can be similar. But what is the cost to my health and to my mental and emotional states when I'm receiving poor care? If the urologist you have now does not test your urine every time you have an infection, why not? If you always get the same antibiotic to treat your bladder infection – why so? For myself, I learned that there are different types of bacteria that respond to different antibiotics. If urine is not tested, then how would a person know what type of antibiotic is needed. We need to invest in the best care available and find doctors who are proactive.

I take antibiotics. I have read reports of other people who are able to clear up bladder infections without taking antibiotics, but that has never been my experience. There is a fine line here, to take antibiotics or not. The goal, the bottom line, for me is to keep my kidneys healthy.

We cannot live without our kidneys. Constant, untreated infections make me unable to interact with my family, friends, and coworkers the way I want to and can ultimately lead to the destruction of my kidneys and the need for dialysis.

But taking antibiotics when they are not needed or failing to

Knowledge Nugget:

The exact cause of Bladder Pain Syndrome is unknown, and scientists have yet to find a cure. They can't predict who will respond to treatment or what treatment is best. Although 80 percent of patients with BPS are women, it usually doesn't occur in families.[5] Symptoms may disappear with a change in diet or treatments—or without any identifiable explanation.[6] Even when symptoms disappear, they may return after days, weeks, months, or years. Additional research on BPS factors could ultimately help with better diagnosistic tests.

Likely Causes:

- the release of histamine (allergic response)
- defects in the cells lining the bladder which become irritated
- specific substances in the urine not found in normal urine
- A change in the nerves that carry bladder sensation, resulting in bladder pain

complete a course of therapy because I feel better after a day or two will increase my chances of contributing to the development of a new, antibiotic-resistant strain of bacteria, a superbug. What a balancing act! This is one reason it's so important to have a doctor I trust guiding my treatment plan.

I let my close associates and family know I am not feeling well. When I am fighting a bladder infection, my energy levels and attitude suffer. The people I work with do not need to know every detail about my health, but they at least deserve an explanation of why I am not up to par. Given all the bugs that travel through a school's hallways, usually I am not the only person under the weather. We look out for each other.

Of course, I can be more detailed with my family, especially my husband. And usually they are all willing to lend a hand with some of the tasks I ordinarily take care of. We don't often think about it, but accepting help from others so that we can rest and give our bodies a chance to heal is an important part of recovering from any illness.

Bladder Pain Syndrome

Bladder pain does not always mean an infection.

I always look at my urine *every* time I urinate because, although I frequently feel bladder pain, my bladder pain is not always caused by an infection (another reason to get my urine tested when I think I may have an infection). Everything from a defect or leak in the protective lining (epithelium) of the bladder, to an autoimmune reaction or allergies can contribute to bladder pain; it is occasionally found to occur in families[3] and thought to be due to genetic factors. Bladder Pain Syndrome (BPS) is something I live with. I am not sure why it occurs, and medical experts are not sure, either.

Knowledge Nugget:

Bladder Pain Syndrome (BPS) is the new designation for the symptom formerly known as interstitial cystitis. BPS refers to a group of chronic pain conditions, rather than primarily an inflammatory bladder disorder. A BPS diagnosis is based on the patient's perception of bladder-related pain, pressure, or discomfort in combination with at least one urinary symptom[4] (e.g., frequency or the persistent urge to void or a bleeding ulceration of the bladder[3]). A doctor will make the initial assessment by considering the results of a frequency/volume chart, a physical examination, urinalysis, and a urine culture.

Bladder Pain Syndrome is not a rare condition. More than 1.3 million Americans have BPS, and many more are undiagnosed[3]; diagnosis is usually in midlife. Besides being caused by frequent bladder infections, it can be caused by other inflammation to the bladder. Let me tell you about Sophie. She remembers when she first had symptoms of chronic bladder pain. She thought she had a bladder infection, but the tests came back negative. Her doctor prescribed medication. He told her that exercise and eating bland food might help and suggested she try to stay away from soft drinks, coffee, and alcohol. She was offered a diet of pears, cottage cheese, and vanilla milkshakes.

Sophie also started seeing a physical therapist who recommended pelvic floor therapy to strengthen her core muscles. Besides the pain, she had the constant urge to urinate. She finally tried a pain-management clinic. Because of the chronic pain, she was depressed. The clinic helped her manage her depression, and she found healthy ways to cope with the pain. Even though Sophie deals with her bladder pain differently than I do, I have come to understand that I am not the only one who feels bladder pain. Bladder Pain Syndrome is such a mystery. It seems to have many causes. Mine is not as severe as Sophie's. When I get uncomfortable, I am able to keep busy and get distracted. Either way, there are ways to cope, starting with the advice from a doctor.

Sometimes, even when my urine is clear, I feel discomfort. Perhaps this is because knowing where my bladder is located gives me heightened sensitivity. I go on with my day, but I am aware of the sensation in my bladder. When I was first diagnosed with Neurogenic Bladder, I might have used a catheter too often because I mistook my bladder pain for my lost urge to urinate. (Now, rather than depend on feeling physical sensations or worry about not feeling anything at all, I try to time my urination about every three to four hours.) Those of us with Neurogenic Bladder need to pay attention to our bladder pain and consult with our doctors whenever there's a change in our symptoms. We need to listen to our bodies. A change may simply be the result of changes in our bodies as we age. Or it may be a signal of a new medical problem developing that requires immediate treatment. Let's face these situations directly, rather than delaying diagnosis and possibly allowing a serious medical issue to become advanced and more difficult to treat successfully.

Kidneys

Before my diagnosis of Neurogenic Bladder, I gave no thought to my kidneys. Every time I felt back pain, I thought it was a slipped disk. It did not occur to me that upper back pain can indicate kidney issues. When you feel pain on either side of your back, don't assume that the chiropractor is your ticket. Your kidneys could be talking to you.

Now that I have been diagnosed, I can't afford to ignore my kidneys. If I start running a fever while I have a bladder infection, I need to let my doctor know. This can be a sign that the kidneys are involved.

While kidneys can absorb a lot of abuse (they are so redundant that many people live just fine with only one kidney), they are not invincible. Ignoring bladder infections can cause long-term kidney damage, leading to a need for dialysis or transplant.

We can strengthen our kidneys through our diet. The best foods for kidneys are bell peppers, blueberries, cabbage, cauliflower, cherries, cranberries, egg whites, fish, garlic, olive oil, onions, raspberries, red grapes, and strawberries. And don't forget the water.

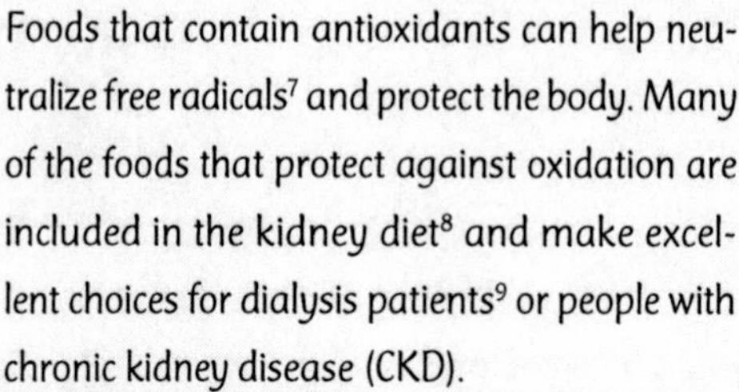

Knowledge Nugget:

Foods that contain antioxidants can help neutralize free radicals[7] and protect the body. Many of the foods that protect against oxidation are included in the kidney diet[8] and make excellent choices for dialysis patients[9] or people with chronic kidney disease (CKD).

All of these issues involving bladder infections, Bladder Pain Syndrome, and kidney function may seem like a bit much to absorb. And some days they are. But the nature of Neurogenic Bladder, as is true for other chronic conditions, is that it can impact all of life. The trick to living with a chronic condition is to accept that it affects our lives but not to let it totally control our lives.

5. Intimacy

"My beloved is mine and I am his. He feedeth among the lilies."

—Song of Solomon 2:16 (KJV)

Conceivably one of the areas of life most affected by Neurogenic Bladder is sexual intimacy. When I was first diagnosed, I was afraid to have sex. Because I was new to using a catheter, I was sore in that area anyway. The last thing I wanted was any more activity that would irritate already inflamed tissue. And cathing was not like using a tampon during a menstrual period. It did not intrude on five days a month. It happened several times a day, every single day, stretching out into eternity.

The truth is I was losing my sense of identity. I'd always thought of myself as a healthy, active, sexy wife. But feeling sexy when I was in pain and struggling to get used to catheterizing myself was more than I could handle most days. It took all I had to paste on a smile and tell myself, "You are sexy!"

Sometimes I wondered if the diagnosis of Neurogenic Bladder and Bowel would ultimately change my marital relationship. Would this disease affect my nerves to the point where I never experienced the bells and whistles of orgasm again? When would the next shoe drop? What would I lose next? Would I lose the ability to weep with pleasure?

When my husband got that sparkle in his eye, I wanted to cry. I felt broken and already used. Perhaps I felt raped by the stupid catheters. I did not want to traumatize myself further.

Bladder infections were the bane of my existence, and I wanted to avoid them at all costs. So much medical advice stressed that people who got frequent bladder infections should urinate after intercourse to flush any bacteria out of the urogenital cavity. Well, what if I had to catheterize myself? How did that help? Would sex make things worse?

I was too shy to discuss these issues with my doctor, something that would have ultimately made this transition much easier for me. I did not want to draw attention to my concerns regarding sex and my sexuality. Maybe, on some level, I hoped that, if I did not talk about my personal health issues, even with my husband, I would figure it out on my own, or they would just disappear. Of course, I did not, and they did not, either. So instead, for too long, I lived alone with my fears and questions.

The thought of getting a bladder infection from having sex caused me to shut down. Instead of being pouty because of the rejection, my husband patiently – and I cannot emphasize enough how patiently – pressed on. I was so afraid of getting sicker. I felt like saying, "I already gave at the office, so leave me alone." It was the worst sort of mind game.

Fortunately, my husband and I were able to trust each other about this, too. Because of his loving nature and openness to my concerns, he helped me to express my fears and be honest about what I needed from him in order to be comfortable having sex. We discussed issues of hygiene that are so important when dealing with Neurogenic Bladder. We talked about how almost constant pelvic pain made it more difficult to find that sweet spot and how it might take longer to warm up. In addition, I realized that I needed to be careful about overthinking issues. If I allowed fear to control me, I might be alive, but I would not be living.

Basic Guidelines for Intimacy

The pleasures of sex are a wonder, but we should consider some rules of thumb when dealing with damaged and paralyzed parts. These suggestions are based on my personal experience and conversations with my doctors, and I encourage you to discuss these issues with your urologist or, if you feel more comfortable, with your gynecologist so you can benefit from her expertise and knowledge of your individual medical issues and concerns. If it would be helpful, your doctor could recommend a sex therapist to help you and your partner "work around" the physical challenges that your condition creates. Therapists can also help us deal with fear and other emotions that may keep us from enjoying sex.

Some positions are less problematic with regard to comfort and contamination of the urethra from exposure to the penis and sperm.

The female urethra is toward the front, so it poses little risk of exposing the vagina to urine during intercourse. The whole missionary-position joke has some truth to it as far as determining what is safe. The woman stands less chance of picking up an infection from incidental contact when her partner faces her.

Feces are filled with bad bacteria, so think twice before using some creative positions. Saliva is likewise filled with bacteria, so care may be needed in how oral sex is incorporated in intimacy. If a particular technique introduces any chance of getting a bit of feces or saliva near the urethra, where it can move into the bladder, then watch out: a bladder infection is very likely to happen.

Constipation can cause discomfort during intercourse, so don't forget to help things along, if necessary.

Procedures for sterile catheterization must be maintained. Because an intermittent catheter pushes through the tube of the urethra and up to the neck of the bladder, it could inadvertently cause infection, especially if any bacteria are either near the urethra or clinging to the catheter. To further protect from infection, take a shower or use your peri bottle to cleanse following any sexual activity and before you even consider using your sterile catheter.

Use prescription hormone cream if approved by your doctor. Prescription hormone cream helps make the labia of postmenopausal women become thicker and healthier when applied several times a week. It wards off infection and also helps with arousal.

Don't assume that pain eliminates the possibility of intimacy. All situations are different, and we experience pain on different levels. At times, pain is so great that it's an absolute block to anything more than perhaps being held gently. And no one should ever feel forced to do something that causes or increases pain. But sometimes working through the pain can produce positive results. In some ways, sex might be like running a marathon. It can be hard to start. It is easy to overthink all the obstacles that may appear and be tempted to quit at the first sign of a problem. However, as a couple patiently persists, the body begins to feel relaxation and pleasure, and the pain begins to subside. In the end, the endorphins and positive feelings make you feel so happy that you ran the race.

Don't get obsessed with achieving intercourse. There is more to sex than intercourse. We can reach orgasm through many other ways of pleasuring each other. What's important is the act of loving, the act of caring, and the opportunity to celebrate each other.

Benefits of Intimacy

Now, this is the best part: there are great benefits to orgasm itself[1].

Orgasm can strengthen connections to our partner. The biggest benefit that I see is the spiritual bonding that takes place between my husband and me. We become soul mates in every way: he is mine and I am his.

The stretching and moving during an orgasm does the body good! At times, I become stiff and sore. But after our special time together, I feel great pain relief and a sense of relaxation. I am sure the endorphins help my feeling of calm and wellbeing. I sleep better, too.

Tip Time:

Be honest with your partner about how he or she can be supportive and patient.

Try not to overthink.

Be willing to laugh.

Know about products such as hormone creams that can prevent bladder infections and help with arousal.

Take a shower together.

Be creative and try new things.

Be willing to talk with medical professionals about your concerns.

Consider pushing past the pelvic pain.

It helps with the overall cleansing of our bodies. Our lymph nodes help to detoxify our bodies. One of the ways they are emptied is by the type of movement that takes place during orgasm.

During orgasm, many hormone levels spike which help brain function: Oxytocin, often considered the hormone for effective people because it helps a person feel content. Estrogen keeps the vaginal area supple and helps ward off bladder infections. Orgasm even releases a growth hormone that helps us stay young. Now, don't we all want that?

Orgasm is good for the heart. I well recall the scene in *Private Benjamin* where Goldie's husband dies in the act. Fear not. As long as you and your partner have a doctor's assurance that you are healthy enough for sex, then orgasm could be good for your heart. It even lowers your blood pressure.

Besides that, consider the extra calories you are using. "Better than the gym," I say. In life, we need to use it or lose it. Go for it!

The most frequently viewed post from my blog is the one on sex. This does not surprise me one bit. We are all sexual beings, and God has given us a marvelous gift. But because of nerve damage in our pelvic regions, some of us need to work a little harder to keep this gift going, and sometimes it does not feel so much like a gift but more like a job.

I hate to think what my life might be like now if my husband and I had given in to my fears and physical limitations and simply stopped being physically intimate. An important part of our relationship, of what makes us the couple we are, would have been eliminated unnecessarily.

Just remember: where there is a will, there is a way. My husband was both patient and understanding. We listened to each other, and together we worked through my fears and past my pain. What could have been a great frustration and source of pain in our marriage became an opportunity to learn more about each other and to see our love and appreciation for each other grow. And when we finally broke through, did the bells and whistles ever go off!

On days when we just hurt, it is easy to want to quit. I am here to be your encourager: don't give up! We humans crave touch and need the warmth of another person. We love to love. The fact that some of us suffer from Neurogenic Bladder does not change that truth. I know how scary and difficult it can be to work through the issues of intimacy unique to Neurogenic Bladder. But the benefits intimacy brings to our relationships and to our physical and emotional health are so worth the extra effort. Don't passively accept the loss of intimacy. Reach out to your partner and together create the joy and pleasure in one another that you have known before.

6. Conquest over Depression

The spirit of a man will sustain his infirmity;
but a wounded spirit who can bear?

—Proverbs 18:14 (KJV)

How many people know something is physically wrong with them, but either their symptoms are dismissed or tests to diagnose the problems are inconclusive? Not surprisingly, when weeks, then months, and even years of illness pass without a letup in symptoms or a name to place on them, many of us start feeling depressed. That's certainly what happened to me when I was living with undiagnosed Neurogenic Bladder.

Unfortunately, my condition went undiagnosed for years. I often felt depressed. I was very tired and felt physically unwell. Much later I realized I was not physically ill because of depression. I was depressed because I was living with an undiagnosed medical condition, which made me feel exhausted. The constant discomfort zapped my energy level, sometimes catching me off guard. It was hard to tell which happened first: depression or my body's struggle to fight an infection.

Depression is more than having a bad day. The National Institute of Mental Health describes depression this way: "Everyone occasionally feels blue or sad. But these feelings are usually short-lived and pass within a couple of days. When you have depression, it interferes with daily life and causes pain for both you and those who care about you. Depression is a common but serious illness.[1]"

Knowledge Nugget:

According to the National Institute of Mental Health, these are the most common symptoms of depression[1]:

Persistent sad, anxious, or "empty" feelings

Feelings of hopelessness or pessimism

Feelings of guilt, worthlessness, or helplessness

Irritability, restlessness

Loss of interest in activities or hobbies once pleasurable, including sex

Fatigue and decreased energy

Difficulty concentrating, remembering details, and making decisions

Insomnia, early-morning wakefulness, or excessive sleeping

Overeating or appetite loss

Thoughts of suicide, suicide attempts

Aches or pains, headaches, cramps, or digestive problems that do not ease, even with treatment.

Depression affects people in different ways. When I feel depressed, food is not appealing, jokes are not funny, and colors seem muted. My symptoms are both physical and emotional. It affects my whole being. For me, depression was related to my Neurogenic Bladder and the loss of control of my body and, therefore, what I perceived to be my life.

Dangers of Isolation

In my situation, discovering the cause of my health problems was liberating. Once I knew I had Neurogenic Bladder, I wanted to learn everything I could about it, but my mind also swirled with self-doubt. I was horrified at the thought of others' knowing about my condition, even my family. Shame filled my life because the whole situation seemed so much bigger than I could handle on my own. The isolation of being alone with my thoughts, with no outlet, was simply too much. I was overwhelmed by the fear that I could not manage my health condition and continue my busy lifestyle.

> **Tip Time:**
>
> *Regardless of the factors that may be contributing to your depression, please consult with your doctor or a licensed therapist to get help in finding the causes and determining what can be done to control your depression. I understand that some days simply getting out of bed can be a major accomplishment, but the sooner treatment for depression begins, the more effective it is. If you have suicidal thoughts, don't wait. Call 9-1-1 to receive immediate support.*

On the other hand, I had a pressing urge to come up with solutions. Now that I knew that this condition would be forever, I did not want to be its victim. I wanted to be in charge.

I kept my bladder pain to myself, as well as my ever-present problem of finding a private restroom and receptacle where I could discreetly discard used catheters. Even in my own home, I had a disposal problem. I decided to accessorize my bathroom with a large, lidded garbage can that opens with a foot control, big enough to suffice until the end of the week, when my garbage went out. It also acted as a tabletop to help with my toileting aids since I do not have a counter in my lavatory.

My Breakthrough

Finding peace and real help for my depression and isolation started by taking the step of journaling. Writing about my dilemma was the only outlet I had. I journaled because I felt I had no one I could talk to. I filled pages with how I felt physically and emotionally, sometimes as letters, sometimes as prayers.

Tip Time:

Catheters can take up a lot of space in your bathroom. A larger trash can with a lid that opens with your foot can serve two purposes: it can cover the evidence of the catheters, papers, and all the plastic we use, and act as a working surface area if you need one.

This isolation I felt was, of course, unfounded. The sad thing is that I did have some people in my life who would have been willing to listen to me, but I was just too embarrassed to confide in them. I was afraid I would become the butt of jokes rather than the recipient of much-needed support and sympathy. I wanted them to understand the magnitude of how bad I was feeling and how having a Neurogenic Bladder and Bowel was not as funny as seen in the media.

During this mind-blowing time, I took a writing class. The teacher encouraged me to journal. She gave us ideas for keeping the tools of the trade handy: our computers, pens and paper, and encouraged us to let our thoughts come – to put them in a place where they would not be gone forever. For our assignments, I turned in pages and pages of my thoughts. I wrote about being embarrassed by voiding situations. I wrote about the doctors I appreciated and some that I did not. I scripted ideas of how I could carry my catheters safely around.

As I processed the information I was garnering about myself, I got a clearer picture of what I needed to do to cope with my newfound medical condition. My shame was lessening because, instead of running from it, I began embracing it. I still did not know how to get past my fear of being ridiculed if I confided in someone I knew. I could reveal things to my writing teacher because she was a stranger and was reading my thoughts in my absence rather than listening to me face-to-face. The situation felt much less threatening than talking directly with a family member or friend.

Beginning to Connect

I was hooked on writing. I moved my journal to an anonymous blog format, thanks to the help and ease of using Typepad, my first online blogging tool. I had few computer or writing skills, and I was an even worse speller. However, I did have thoughts to share, so I pressed on. Anonymity was key: I was still too humiliated to share all of my symptoms openly with my doctors, let alone with my friends or even my husband. The accidents that happened in public places were too raw to share directly with anyone.

> **Tip Time:**
>
> *Sometimes, reactions are far from ideal. Loved ones may be embarrassed by your revelation. Perhaps they snicker because they don't really understand. A few, if they really thought about it, would offer compassion and an "Atta boy" slap on the shoulder. Talking about it is just way too hard. Offer Grace.*

In the early days of the blog, I mostly wrote about things I was having a hard time discussing with anyone else. I got a funny e-mail from a reader who said, "I can't believe you write about this stuff." But I needed an outlet, and, through the Internet, I found others who understood the emotional prison in which I found myself. I found solace by sharing how I coped with even the basic logistics of my chronic illness.

I decided to choose a pen name because I was too humiliated to use my own name. I picked "Trudy" because a childhood friend had a really nice big sister by that name. She was always kind to us little kids, put up with our tagging along, and enjoyed listening to our chatter. She even married a doctor. So, as the new Trudy, I would be armed with medical knowledge to tear into this Goliath of a topic that threatened to overwhelm my life.

Then the most amazing thing happened. As I blogged about my condition and started learning about others in similar situations, I started feeling normal again. I became less humiliated by my physical challenges. I started getting e-mails from women like me who felt like they were at the end of their ropes. Before I was diagnosed, I did not realize that many paraplegics have nonworking bladders and bowels. I did not know that bladder infections could hurt so much and, more importantly, I did not know I would ever, in a million years, meet such amazing and inspiring people through my own bladder and bowel issues.

The Importance of Research

I started feeling better about myself. In the process of writing the blog, I had to research Neurogenic Bladder and Bowel and not only learned more about the topic but also became more comfortable with myself. I realized that, within the larger scheme of things, my symptoms of Neurogenic Bladder were a lot milder than those that many others had to live with.

I also quickly understood that I was not alone. From my blog readers, I learned that a lot of extra suffering is caused by the lack of understanding and sympathy for our condition and by doctors who are vague.

I also learned that Neurogenic Bladder and Bowel are relatively common among women, especially those who have had vaginal deliveries.

I discovered a very interesting study on a group of people with spinal-cord injuries who needed to cath. In total, 102 women and men participated (ages eighteen to seventy-five). They all completed the Beck Depression Inventory (BDI) and their results were compared to the results of people who were free to urinate, any time, anyhow [Oh SJ, 2006]. Patients with Neurogenic Bladder due to spinal-cord injuries had higher degrees of depression than the general population. The subjects' depression was also closely related to gender (women had a higher rate). Not surprisingly, those subjects able to self-catheterize were less depressed than those who required help. In order to rule out depression that might be caused by something other than the need to catheterize, this study excluded people with MS, Parkinson's disease, diabetic atrophy, AIDS, or any other disease that causes symptoms in addition to Neurogenic Bladder. The study looked exclusively at whether and how much cathing and Neurogenic Bladder led to depression.

I did not come to accept my "new normal" overnight. Those of us who develop a chronic condition go through a grieving process because we have lost some of our health as well as our ability to do some things that we enjoy. Depression is one of the steps many grieving people go through before they reach a point of acceptance.

All of this research helped me understand that feeling depressed was a normal reaction to my physical condition. And, while I'm fortunate enough to have a disposition that's inclined to look at the bright side, sometimes life with Neurogenic Bladder is tough. There's no escaping that fact. When someone suggests "doing something about it," I sometimes want to shout, "I am dressed, aren't I?"

Knowledge Nugget:

In their book *The Overactive Bladder,* K. Kreder and R. Dmochowski[2] note, "Overactive bladder (OAB) affects millions of men and women daily. Given the symptoms of sleep loss, depression, and a lower quality of life than even those with diabetes mellitus, effective and beneficial treatment is a must..."

Family and Friends

Just as I needed time to adjust to my physical condition, the close family members and friends with whom I shared my condition needed time to come to grips with everything that this change meant. First, some people are not capable of "being there" for those of us with physical limitations, and all the wishing in the world is not going to change this. We need to accept them as they are and not demand from them support they are not able to provide. Second, some people will initially respond in ways that may not be helpful or may even feel like personal rejection. Given time, however, they can become some of our fiercest defenders and protectors.

I usually spend a lot of time on the phone with my sister, who is, in many ways, my best friend. We played together as kids and ended up having our children at the same time. You'd think she knows everything about me. Well, no, she just is not that interested in even thinking about Neurogenic Bladder and Bowel. Why? The subject matter, of course! She'd rather be kept in the dark.

Sometimes I don't feel like being stoic while talking to her. Sometimes I want to answer her question, "How are you?" with the truth. I feel like exploding with drama and emotion. I get tired of putting on a happy face. My feelings are raw, and I would like to be honest with my sister about my life with Neurogenic Bladder. There is more to me than meets the eye, and I want to share all of it: the good, the bad, and the ugly. Just once, I would like to call my sister and tell her all about the trauma I endured getting stuck in the grocery line and being late to the privy.

Most people I know and love do not care to hear about such details of this part of my life. But that does not mean they don't care about me or are indifferent to my suffering. In fact, some of these same people, including my sister, can be more attuned to my needs than I am. She and her husband met my husband and me in San Francisco. We were outside Candlestick Park, waiting for a trolley car to take us to Fisherman's Wharf, a local tourist attraction. Just before the next trolley was due to arrive, my brother-in-law said something really funny. I laughed so hard that it made me really need to urinate. I mentioned something about it. Quick as lightning, my sister said, "Let's go."

At that moment, she knew me better than I knew myself. On my own, I probably would not have left that line because I did not want to miss the next trolley. The consequences could have been disastrous. My sister recognized what I really needed. Despite wanting to be kept in the dark about the details of my condition, she had my back when I needed it. I love her for that!

There are instances when we need to reveal our private life to our family and those woven close to us. It can be awkward because at times responses can be far from ideal. Honest, well-meaning, but incredulous people may have frank reactions. When we candidly explain our medical conditions to them, they may be shocked, embarrassed, or at a loss to respond gracefully. When I remember how stunned I was as I wrapped my head around my diagnosis, it is quite unfair of me to think others should have a tranquil comeback. We all need acceptance for who we are. That goes both ways. I have found it liberating for those close to me to understand my status quo. When the catheters fall out of my pocket as I run down the street or if I am in a public restroom with no trash can in the stall, personally the fear factor is gone when my companions understand my situation. The clumsy setting is no big deal. I can walk out and throw away what I need to throw away or turn around and pick up the dropped catheters. The stress-out is gone and life goes on as normal.

If our nearest and dearest don't understand our special needs, they may misinterpret our behavior, be hurt, or even be insulted when we dash off to use the toilet; reading the situation as a signal that we do not care about what they are saying. The pained look of enduring another bladder infection is just that, nothing more. When inviting us to an activity that seems impossible on that particular day, they understand that it is only temporary, not a forever situation. Understanding that our response," it just won't work" certainly does not mean that something else is more important than they are. This perception helps our chums know that the reason we can't keep pace, has nothing to do with a reluctance to spend time. It has to do with "living logistics at that moment."

At times, I still confront the ugly face of depression but not nearly as often as I used to. My attitude has changed because I better understand why my body behaves like it does, because I have learned to be more open with my doctors, and because I became more willing to share my experiences through my blog and with trusted family and friends. Instead of retreating into shame and isolation, I have learned to accept their support and belief in me and the strength that comes from my faith. My hope is that those who suffer from Neurogenic Bladder and Bowel find hope, acceptance of themselves, and gain strength and self-confidence.

Combatting the Blues

While feelings of depression can at times be unavoidable, I have learned that inactivity and poor food choices can also set me up for being depressed. As much as possible, I work to avoid those triggers, and I make time for activities that help prevent or ease my blue moods.

Now I know that if I start to get those forlorn feelings, I may have a bladder infection coming on. First thing to do is to check it out and, if necessary, get help from my doctor. If I don't have an infection, I have a choice. I can give into my misery and go to bed, or I can take steps to try to pull myself out of that gloominess.

I exercise. I so enjoy walking with my neighbor, using my gym membership, and hiking with my husband. I have a bike I love to ride, and a game of golf here and there also fills the bill.

I do not want to mislead you. Physical activity is hard for me sometimes. My muscles ache, and I get sore. Despite the discomfort, I like the way it makes me feel even if I know I will be sore afterward. Since I live with a chronic illness, sometimes I hurt. I am tempted to pick up a book, but instead I am making that deliberate decision to get out and move my body. I do understand that, if I do not move my body and give in to the lethargy that feels fine for the moment, I will even feel stiffer and sorer the next day from just sitting around. A walking buddy or an appointment at the gym provides the accountability that really helps.

Exercise lifts my mood even if I am sore. I find that, for the rest of the day, I feel more ambitious and, yes, less depressed.

I try to get a good night's sleep. Activity during the day helps me rest at night. I try not to stay out too late on work nights since I get up early. I have found that my body does not bounce back so well with little sleep. When I go out for evening activities on a work night, I have a rule to leave at 8:30 p.m. Sometimes my departure time is in the middle of a really important activity, but I do it anyway. I hold fast because I know that if I am going to be a good worker at school the next day, I need my sleep. I carve that time out, and I am thankful the next day.

I work at being a friend and helping others. I have found that the best way to make a friend is to be a friend. Be a good listener. Find out what is valuable to the person I am befriending and spend time together on a common interest. Invite the person out for an activity; offer to help with that wallpaper.

When we work together, friendships form. Is there a young mother I can help by babysitting? Kids are great for keeping my mind dynamic, and they offer lots of physical activity as well. Can I volunteer at a hospital or church? All of these types of activities take my thoughts off myself and get me involved with others.

Truthfully, I sometimes have problems with socializing in general. I can be perfectly content by myself, yet I know that relationships with others are key to my healthy life. When I extend myself, I see a part of me that I did not know, and I am uplifted by the time spent.

I benefit from hobbies and creating works of art. At different times in my life, I have decorated all the rooms of my home. Special craft projects such as quilting, drawing, painting, and counted cross-stitch give me great joy. Outdoor projects such as gardening are fun, as well. The feeling of satisfaction that comes with making my surroundings a better place helps ward off depression.

Go light on the alcohol. Don't get me wrong. I like my glass of wine now and then, but heavy drinking of wine, beer, and/or liquor causes problems. Studies have shown that too much alcohol does cause despair and that people who are depressed sometimes try to drive that feeling away through substance abuse. It does not work.

I have faith, which gives me hope. If you are reading this, chances are you have lost your bladder function and perhaps your bowel function, as well. Maybe someone you love is in this situation, and you want to offer hope as well as be done with the worry you carry for your loved one. I wish our earthly life was that simple. While some people experience loss of bladder and bowel function for a short time, they are the lucky ones. Most of us will live with this loss for the rest of our lives. And the harsh reality for some is that this is the beginning of the loss of all their bodily functions.

While living with this reality every day, I do not fall into despair, because my faith in God helps keep me grounded, with my head held high. I have hope of a future in heaven. I will spend eternity with a perfect body. I have an eager expectation that my Lord will be honored in how I live my life, despite my circumstances. I try to remember that, when my life is turned upside down, my Lord has my back – that God promises to take my brokenness and make something good from it. My affliction causes me to direct my gaze to him. My inconvenience builds my faith. As my body fails, I try to remember that the battle for the real me, my soul, is already won. I am victorious.

7. A Frank and Honest Look at Devices and Aids

The greatest glory in living lies not in never falling,
but in rising every time we fall.

—Nelson Mandela[1]

Perhaps because of the general discomfort most people experience when discussing bodily functions, we rarely hear experts talk about incontinence. To his credit, on January 7, 2010, Dr. Mehmet Oz devoted an entire show to this subject. He called it the number-one health secret that women keep and identified two major causes of incontinence:

Stress incontinence,[2] which is the most common, is caused by weak muscles. Dr. Oz suggested childbirth and being overweight as two causes for this condition.

Urge incontinence is caused by nerves that don't work so well due to diabetes, trauma, and other neurologically damaging situations. He recommended Kegel exercises, weight loss, bladder retraining, injections, and magnesium, which can help to relax the bladder and is found in pumpkin seeds.

I applaud Dr. Oz for devoting a program to the subject and making viewers aware of how common incontinence issues are. However, perhaps because of the time limitations he faced, he did not address the issues of those of us whose bladder function is permanently disabled. This understanding is an important part of the whole picture.

Incontinence Pads and Diapers

One of the most obvious issues people with Neurogenic Bladder deal with – and unfortunately, one of the greatest sources of frustration – is finding the best bowel- and bladder-accident protection for their needs. No two people are exactly alike, so we can't use one-size-fits-all devices and aids. What's best for leakage will not work for a full-on flood. So for "the rest of the story," I interviewed Scott Beckert, RN, an expert in the field of incontinence products, having worked with patients living with all types of urinary incontinence. He explained that, by default, many of us go to the grocery store and buy an adult brand of protection from stocking clerks who have no idea what we need. They sell us their own brand suited to a woman who dribbles, not a full drencher. The diapers in the store may be geared to light incontinence. What if a person needs help for overnight incontinence? Then a person should use a product that can contain the amount of urine that is expelled overnight. Buying an inferior product can cause frustration and perhaps disaster.

The search for the perfect adult diaper or pad is daunting because there are so many products available and so many factors to consider. It is important to be well informed of your options.[3,4] Scott recommends that first we look for gender-appropriate supplies. Men and women are different, and it matters. How and where the urine enters the product makes a difference in how efficiently it is absorbed.

Incontinence levels vary from person to person, and different types of products are capable of handling different absorption needs. Modern diapers and pads use a combination of super-absorbent, acrylic, acid-based polymers, or SAP, to absorb urine and wick the fluid away from the body. Dry polymers can look like table salt or small beads, but when they get wet, these polymers can hold up to twelve hundred times their mass in fluid and feel more gel-like. Most products are marked with an absorbency guide, which can vary from one manufacturer to another and gives an idea of what urine load the product can most effectively handle. There are numerous absorbent-underwear products that one can buy. Experiment, and find the one that works best for you.

Another concern is how to be discreet while wearing these products (and while buying them), but I will come to this a bit later. Older types of disposable incontinence protection relied heavily on an outer plastic layer, causing the product to crackle and make noise. Who wants that distraction or embarrassment? Today we can find all sorts of body-close products made of nonwoven materials, similar to interfacing fabric, as back sheets, and much thinner and smaller pads that are as sound discreet as cotton or nylon underwear. Some products have an inner core that reduces the amount of acidity in the urine, thus destroying the odor-producing bacteria and making the diaper smell fresh – a good idea when you know you need to be out for a long time. These modern technologies help decrease the potential for noise and embarrassment. Many products do not fit correctly: they are too stiff, feel way too loose around the legs, and do little to protect your clothes. Those old, noisy briefs are now sold as bid items for big contracts. So if someone offers them to you . . . run! Much better options are on the market today. Do not settle for something that does not work.

A fine line exists between providing enough protection and having unnecessary bulk showing under your clothes. A sure way to help with fit is to wear a brief-style underwear over your diaper or pad because it soothes the surface, so your clothes will form-fit.

The quality of the diaper is not necessarily directly reflected in its cost. Nor are diapers or briefs the only things that absorb. How about sanitary napkins? For some women, they are a fantastic solution. Discreet bladder-protection products are specifically designed to handle urine, a thinner/less viscous fluid than menstrual fluid. Going to a retail store to find the right product can be frustrating because of the limited selection and the lack of trained staff. It's best to go to a vendor who specializes in the product and explain exactly the type of incontinence you have. Then you can be paired with a product that will suit your needs.

I have found that talking to an online salesperson about my needs is most helpful. He or she is an expert in the field, and there is the added bonus of much-needed privacy. Make sure that the product you order online or over the phone includes discreet packaging. No need for your neighbors or the mailman to know your business.

We may feel at the mercy of salespeople when purchasing our devices and other medical and hygiene supplies. While most are reliable, some will try to make a sale instead of providing the best product for us. Be wary. Adult diapers are pretty expensive, so if you buy a box that does not work out, it can be an expensive mistake. When I have had questions regarding adult diapers, I found that asking people in online support groups has been my best source of information. These people were so honest and nonjudgmental and truly experts in living life. They use those incontinence products every day. If you are unable to connect with a support group right away I recommend you find yourself a reputable supplier who has real experience in the incontinence industry and ask for help. Your insurance company can tell you who their preferred providers are for these supplies, and some doctors' offices will help you with this, as well.

Explain your situation and your needs to the supplier. Be specific. Most of the time, salespeople will be trustworthy and help you get what you need. They may ask questions to help provide better assistance. If you are afraid of buying the wrong item, ask for samples or order one pack at a time instead of a whole case. Scott told me of a woman he worked with in California who ordered several different types and brands at one time for her Mom in Indiana. The daughter did her homework in California, and the Mom figured out just what she needed as she tried them in Indiana. Everyone was happy.

Scott shared with us that his highest-volume customers were families in which the older kids wet the bed. This is a common occurrence. Using the right products can revolutionize a teenager's social life.

Skin irritation can be a problem as well. Diaper rash can be avoided by limiting the exposure of your skin to urine and fecal matter. Change as frequently as you can, and try to keep your skin dry. Cloth diapers need to be changed as soon as they are wet. Disposable diapers tend to do better if you need to wear the diaper for a long time. Make sure they fit properly to prevent their rubbing on the skin. Use a protective barrier or a cream cleanser such as TENA Wash Cream, Desitin, and zinc oxide or Baza Cream to protect skin from the urine and feces until it is possible to change the brief. Make sure the skin is cleansed and dried between diaper changes. Leaving urine and feces on the skin can leave enzymes that will break down the skin.

The first plan of attack should be to keep clean and dry and not get a rash, but if one develops, use a rash cream sparingly. The creams do not wash off easily, and, if the cream is applied too liberally, it can impede the absorption of the diaper,

Another product that can cause irritation is perfumed soap and water. Disposable products that are easier on the skin are available. If you develop sensitivities to materials used in your product, consult your supplier. A reputable company will be able to help you find another option that works.

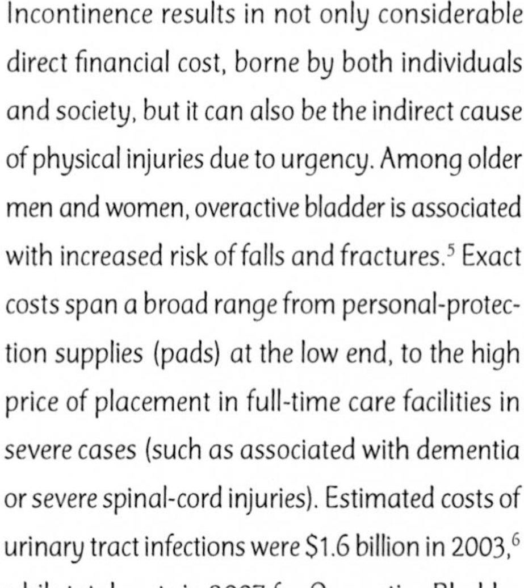

Knowledge Nugget:

Incontinence results in not only considerable direct financial cost, borne by both individuals and society, but it can also be the indirect cause of physical injuries due to urgency. Among older men and women, overactive bladder is associated with increased risk of falls and fractures.[5] Exact costs span a broad range from personal-protection supplies (pads) at the low end, to the high price of placement in full-time care facilities in severe cases (such as associated with dementia or severe spinal-cord injuries). Estimated costs of urinary tract infections were $1.6 billion in 2003,[6] while total costs in 2007 for Overactive Bladder were estimated at $65.9 billion in the U.S.[7]

Toilet seats

Big John Toilet Seat

We may not think about our toilet seats in terms of managing our condition, but they can actually make a significant difference in the ease with which we use certain devices and in our ability to keep as clean as possible. Big John toilet seats are made to accommodate people weighing up to one thousand pounds. While I weigh nowhere near that, I must confess I would never be without my Big John. The model I use has an opening in front and is raised quite a bit, giving me a straight shot when I use a catheter. It also helps me stay cleaner, a big help since I am prone to bladder infections.

> **Tip Time:**
>
> *Although toilets are not really considered a medical device, having a good one does make our lives easier. I highly recommend you try a toilet seat that is raised high and wide for easy access.*

It took a while to get used to the Big John, because I felt like a bird perched up on a branch, but I am truly grateful for the convenience it offers me. I learned about it on a Facebook page with posts from other people living with Neurogenic Bladder and Bowel problems. With their encouragement, I sought one out, and I am so glad I did.

Catheters

If you hoped this section would be filled with information about the choices of catheters we can use, I am sorry to disappoint you. However,

I would like to share with you what I have learned about locating and purchasing the right one. Unfortunately, we can't just buy catheters at the local drugstore. We are therefore either at the mercy of the new flavor of the month at the doctor's office or responsible for finding and maintaining our supply, which must be readily on hand.

That process can be a bit more complicated than we would wish. Several times, I tried to go online and take advantage of a free offer of catheters that I had seen in a television ad. I was told to send my prescription, and they would send samples right away. After receiving the sample product, I found I had confused my insurance carrier because it thought I wanted to buy from the "free offer" sales representative on a continous basis.

The best sources I have found for information on selection and purchasing options of urinary catheters have been online support groups and the urological nurses at my urologist's office. They are the most open about discussing what works. Personally, I use a lubricated, ready-to-use catheter. It is relatively

Knowledge Nugget:

"Medical- and surgical-supply companies are set up to bill insurance plans for equipment covered by policies, whereas most pharmacies are not set up to do so. Most pharmacies don't have the staffing or knowledge to do the billing, which also requires a contract with the supply source. Pharmacies will, however, try to help patients by providing local sources for obtaining medical supplies upon request. It is up to the patient to decide if they want to deal with a supply company in person or through mail order, but options do exist."

—Jennifer Newman (Registered pharmacist, Washington State, staff pharmacist with more than twenty-five years of experience), personal communication, October 28, 2013.

expensive, but it is worth it for me. Some women think the catheter I just love is too short. Yet it works perfectly for me.

I would love to see more types of catheters sold in drug stores to make it convenient for those of us who need them daily. As the Baby Boomers age, more of us will need toileting aids. They sell diapers in the drugstore, so why not catheters?

Inserting an Intermittent Urinary Catheter

I find it a bit surprising that so many articles tell women to use a mirror when inserting a catheter. When I read directions like this, I suspect a man wrote it because men really can see their private parts and perhaps don't stop to think that women cannot – or even consider the fact that we might run out of hands while inserting a catheter *and* holding a mirror.

So, here is how to insert a catheter without looking. The key is to understand the anatomy in the female genital area (vulva). The clitoris kind of stands out on its own. The vagina is the large opening behind the clitoris. The urethral opening is between the clitoris and the vaginal opening.

I start by washing my hands with soap. The catheter I use is self-lubricated, so that takes out a big step. If I accidentally touch the tip of my catheter with my hand or another object, I throw it away, to prevent infection. I do not clean my labia at the time of insertion, since I shower once a day. My urologist told me it is not necessary, anyway.

There is another school of thought, and that is that cleaning your labia with an antibiotic solution before using a catheter is best. My thoughts on this vary. I know there are bacteria in the labia, but the stinging that can happen if I had to put a solution on my labia six times a day makes me "ouch" just thinking about it. For advice about this, ask your doctor.

After washing your hands, gently press the catheter in the area between the clitoris and the vaginal opening, and soon you will find the spot. There is definitely an opening, which will become apparent as you probe gently. It will happen, I promise.

After I use my catheter, I throw it away because reusing catheters can cause bladder infections. If at all possible, I suggest you use a single-use catheter.

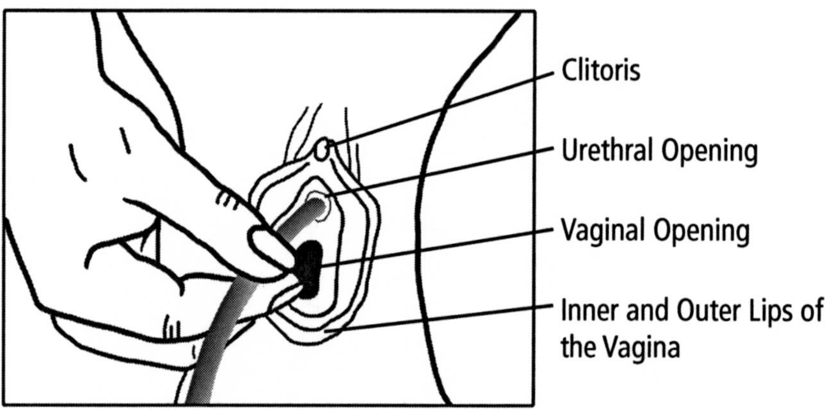

A Woman's Vulva and Insertion of Woman's Intermittent Catheter.
Illustrated by Robin Black

Slimy Tubes and Tricky Situations

When I am gallivanting around, I carry my catheters in a side pouch. I know this sounds silly, but I am afraid of not having them with me in case the big earthquake hits. Through experience, I have learned that catheters are not easy to dispose of when I am out and about, especially if I am visiting a home where I know the person emptying the garbage, so I carry a zip-lock baggie, which I can just carry out with me. I have a "don't tell" policy; it is easier that way. I can't believe how many public restrooms do not have trash disposal.

Knowledge Nugget:

Advantages of Clean Intermittent Catheterization

Sterile intermittent catheterization was developed in 1947, and, by 1966, a long-term study concluded that this method is state of the art in the management of Neurogenic Bladder. The advantages of clean intermittent catheterization (CIC), which is regarded as the most effective way to aid in bladder-emptying disorders, include a lower risk of urinary tract infections (UTI), urosepsis, and renal damage, besides providing autonomy and mobility.[8,9,10] Prior to the availability of sterile intermittent catheterization, renal failure was one of the most frequent causes of death in spinal-cord injury patients, besides the abnormal backflow of urine back up into the ureters from the bladder (vesico-ureteral reflux). (Pressure within the kidney itself can severely damage it and prevent normal function.) Because urethral catheters are the most frequent cause of UTIs in hospitalized patients,[11] it is important to adopt a system that reduces that risk. Sterile intermittent catheterization, when used long term, reduces renal scarring and bladder calculi (stones),[12] which are common in bladders containing stagnant urine.

Toileting happens wherever you are. Be ready! Living with a Neurogenic Bladder and Bowel means we need to be as prepared as a Girl Scout, as diligent as a new mother, and as ready as an army troop deploying overseas. I always have my catheters along. But there is more to being prepared than just having the material goods, believe me. I needed to train, and so do you.

Every day, sitting on the

Tip Time:

Because I need urinary catheters with me while carrying out daily activities, I have found some stashing places that keep me safe in case I run out and have forgotten to bring them along:

The car glove compartment

The nurse's room at work

Out-of-the-way spot in the kids' or trusted friends' restrooms

All of the restrooms in my home

All first-aid kits should have them, don't you think?

toilet, I insert my catheter quickly and efficiently. I use the same old position. Every day, it is the same angle, the same technique. I don't even think about the insertion point anymore. I do it on autopilot. But what happens if I am out and need to use a really dirty porta-potty or if I am in the wilderness and need to pee in the great outdoors? My body position changes, placing my urethra at some wonky angle. I am sweating bullets because not only do I need to pee, but people are waiting for me, and, for some reason, my catheter is not inserting.

Think about it. Our body evolves during different life stages such as having a baby, being overweight, or being underweight. Our urethral area is not necessarily held into place solidly. Sure, we have a pelvis, but it is a bit like a bowl of jelly. We move, and our body morphs. What works well in one position is impossible in another. So why not consider placing your body in different positions while you cath at home and are not under pressure? You will learn where to insert the catheter when your body is not in its normal position.

It is not always possible to sit on the same toilet or even on a toilet at all. Life takes us all over, and we should not be so willing to give that very precious freedom away because we are afraid of where the next toilet is. Is it more difficult for us? Yes! But let's just get over it, practice other positions to cath ourselves, and get out and have fun.

Tip Time:

A belted pouch with divider pockets allows you to keep your catheters separate from other personal items, ensuring privacy and the sterility of the catheter packaging.

Foley Catheter

In 1932, Frederick Foley redesigned the catheter. In the more than eighty years since then, not much has changed with this overused device, which is connected to an external bag. While intermittent catheterization has proven to be the very best treatment for Urine Retention, the Foley catheter, also called an indwelling catheter because it remains in place for days, is still the "main squeeze" in hospitals and nursing homes. It is considered convenient and easy to use, but for whom?

I have had several surgeries and, because I found it difficult to pee on my own, I was given a Foley catheter in the hospital. Every time I ended up with a UTI. The pain of those infections, as well as the risk they pose to kidneys, should be considered when determining what type of catheter a patient receives. For me, I feel less confined if I am able to do for myself what I am used to doing. If the study above states that, for a short hospital stay, the incidence of bladder infections is the same as for a Foley or intermittent catheter, then, please, just let me do what is normal for me.

Knowledge Nugget:

Researchers in England [Dixon, L. 2010], found both the length of hospital stay and total duration of catheterization were reduced when directly comparing the use of intermittent urethral catheterization with indwelling suprapubic catheterization in women undergoing surgery for urodynamic stress incontinence or uterovaginal (pelvic organ) prolapse. There was no difference in the rate of urinary tract infections between the two groups.

I am not sure Foleys should be mandated when one could use intermittent catheterization, which is associated with lower rates of infection in general for long term. The hospital could be a perfect place to train patients and caregivers in the technique of intermittent catheterization.

So why are nursing homes, rehab facilities, and other similar institutions not doing more intermittent catheterization for the infirm?[16] Because of my propensity for bladder infections, I have given this some thought. Of course, there are situations when an intermittent catheter won't work – for instance when a patient cannot self-cath or there are not enough caregivers to provide cathing assistance on a regular basis. But should not that be the exception, rather than the rule? Why is it, with what we know about the safety of intermittent catheters, that they are not standard fare in hospitals and other health-care facilities? Who stands up for the infirm who are quietly out of sight and suffering from unnecessary infections? I think the standard should be to offer to teach intermittent catheterization to a patient or caretakers if they want to learn instead of only offering the standard Foley catheter.

Sometimes, I forget that what is normal for me in regard to catheters, can be novel to others, even in the medical profession. For example, what started as a simple weekend getaway to the beach turned into anything but during the first bike ride of the day. I crashed and burned and broke my hip. It is one thing to deal with a broken hip, but having a broken hip and a Neurogenic Bladder is one tough cookie.

After spending four hours in the emergency room while the

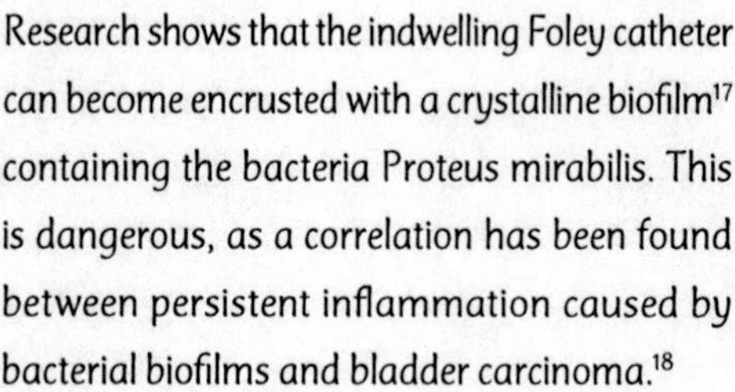

Knowledge Nugget:

Research shows that the indwelling Foley catheter can become encrusted with a crystalline biofilm[17] containing the bacteria Proteus mirabilis. This is dangerous, as a correlation has been found between persistent inflammation caused by bacterial biofilms and bladder carcinoma.[18]

on-call doctor sent X-rays and CT-scans to an orthopedic surgeon for advice, I needed to pee. I explained that I had a Neurogenic Bladder and needed to use a catheter. Because I am a woman, they gave me a bedpan that was really shallow. As the urine flowed and because I had to use one hand for the catheter and try to pivot my body to sit correctly on the bed pan, the shallow bedpan tipped, and urine spilled all over the bed. It was very humbling to have to ask the emergency nurse for a new garment and bedding.

> **Tip Time:**
>
> *If you are offered a shallow bedpan to relieve yourself, ask for a vomit bag or the type of urinal that men get. Do not even try to sit on a bedpan. You do not need it. Women who use catheters can aim and shoot our urine accurately on small areas. Problem solved. Next time I am in an emergency room, which I hope is never again, I will know what equipment to ask for when it comes time to empty my bladder.*

I do not remember much about the three-hour ambulance ride back home in the middle of the night. I arrived at my local hospital and after looking at my medical chart, the doctor ordered a Foley catheter. The next day, the on-call orthopedic surgeon put three pins in my hip to secure the fractured bones. Unknown to me, he told the nurses that the Foley catheter needed to stay in for the duration of my hospital stay. As I woke up from surgery I asked to have the Foley catheter removed. No way. I had to wait until the next day because of the doctor's order.

Of course I understand the doctor's order was given because of the necessity for me to remain very still, and perhaps he did not understand how simple it was for me to relieve myself. It did not occur to me to make arrangements or have something put into my chart about my wish to try to catheterize myself first and to have a Foley inserted only if I could not self-cath.

Sure enough, after I returned home, I needed antibiotics, because I got a bladder infection from the Foley.

Knowledge Nugget:

Physicians working in large medical facilities or institutions strictly follow hospital policies and health-care guidelines since they are tied to accreditation. The health-care policy guidelines they adopt are recommended best medical practices that are in place to provide good medical care. It takes time and multiple studies demonstrating better treatment standards to get policies changed or updated.

For instance, the hospital into which JoAnne was admitted must have had a policy that recommended or required a Foley catheter inserted in any patient having surgery on a broken hip (or other debilitating, long-term care that required a hospital stay). Only by educating policymakers and physicians of the dangers of indwelling catheters and the availability of US-based studies showing the benefits of clean intermittent catheterization (CIC) for those with Neurogenic Bladder will policies likely be changed.

A new policy might recommend that any patient with a preexisting condition that requires regular catheterization should be allowed to choose her catheterization method. In addition, nursing staff would have to be trained to accommodate the process.

Sympathy

During my hospitalization, three of the nurses showed signs of sadness, sympathy, and grave concern when I told them about my Neurogenic Bladder. I must admit their reactions made me feel like a freak of nature instead of a healthy woman getting ready to heal. Their emotional response surprised me. If their sympathy had been about the loss of my vacation and my ability to bicycle for a while, I would not have minded at all having them sit by my bed and cry crocodile tears. I was really feeling sorry for myself at the time, and that act of sympathy would have mirrored my own disappointment and frustration. But the nurses showed me sympathy because of my Neurogenic Bladder. The bladder I will have every day for the rest of my life. The bladder I can do nothing about. The bladder that is normal to me. Their sympathy seemed misguided to me. I was in the hospital as a result of a biking accident and a broken hip, not because of my bladder.

No one who needs to work a little harder to live a "normal" life appreciates being set apart or treated as an object of pity. I work in a school with children who come in all shapes and sizes, and have a wide range of cognitive abilities. We know better than to show sympathy for a student because the life he will live will be based on what he alone is capable of doing. We try to take the students from where they are and build on all the resources they have. We encourage them to work with what they have and be who they are. What they have is perfect for them. Perfection has many faces, because we are all so different.

In any case, the nurses were quite interested in my intermittent catheter and how easy it was to use. I was surprised by this because I assumed that people in medical professions were trained on the very safest procedures, not just the most convenient.

With all of the hype about germs that can abound in a hospital and with hospital administrators reassuring us that they are trying their very best to keep hospital infection down, perhaps they should at least take a look at training their doctors and nursing staff in intermittent catheterization.

Benefits of Using a Woman's Urinary Catheter

There are a few benefits to using a woman's intermittent catheter: I can easily stand to pee, so when I am out and away from home, I do not need to sit in a strange porta-potty. Since I have bladder retention, I can go quite a while before I need to pee. I am kind of like a camel. How convenient! Another advantage is that women my age experience vulvar dryness, yet when I use a catheter, I get a little lubrication, which is a good thing.

Whether we're dealing with catheters, absorbent underwear, diapers, pads, or some other medical device or aid, we need to make sure that our tools work for us, rather than against us. I can't encourage you enough to take the time to find what is best for you. Seek out the professionals who will assist you in this process, and refuse to settle for second best. We have enough variety in our product choices so that *something* should work just right for you. Using tools that solve our problems and make our lives easier is one more way to live independently rather than just survive.

Tip Time:

Even before you go to the hospital, have your doctor put in your chart that you would like to self-cath if at all possible, to avoid infection. If not, ask that the nursing staff use intermittent catheterization employing sterile technique.

8. Living Life Well

God gave us the gift of life;
it is up to us to give ourselves the gift of living well.

—Voltaire[1]

Too often, those of us with chronic illnesses fall into the trap of simply surviving. The real limitations we live with mutate into overwhelming obstacles, keeping us from living life fully. I have found four areas that help me expand my world, and I think they could help you, as well. Please note that some of these Tip Time tips were offered to me by my medical professionals and nutritionists, and some I learned through living with bladder problems. I want to share what has worked for me and suggest that you partner with your medical team to determine what is best for you.

Eating Well

It's worthwhile discussing food when talking about Neurogenic Bladder and Bowel because we really are, in many ways, what we eat. So much of our health is shaped by what we consume.

I learned from an early age that my diet will help me succeed or bring me down. We had great meals growing up. My grandmother lived with us and did most of the cooking. We ate a lot of foods with just one ingredient such as fruits, vegetables, eggs, milk, and meat. I try to eat like that today to keep healthy. My mother was an organic-food nut before I even knew what it was. I begged her for Wonder Bread because all of the other kids got to eat it, but to no avail. And yes, we all ate vegetables; I grew up in Salinas, California, the salad bowl of the world, and my dad worked in agriculture.

Mom regularly passed on advice about our eating.

Food Tips from my Mom:

Note: These Tip Time tips are not completely verbatim, but I grew up hearing them all the same.

Alcohol and sugar can rot your brain. If you want to remain clearheaded, stay away from both.

Eat fruit and veggies every day.

Eat breakfast every day.

Wait until dinner.

Eat an orange at the beginning of the day, even before coffee.

Clean with vinegar and water. If you can eat it, it will not poison your skin.

When you buy grapes, buy them with seeds. Then chew the entire grape up.

Put a piece of bread in your mouth when you cut an onion so your eyes won't tear.

Eating well does not always come naturally. We face so many temptations. But we also have supplements and special foods that can really help us stay on track. I visited a naturopathic doctor to learn more about how I can help my body stay strong as I live with Neurogenic Bladder and Bowel. Here are some tips that she shared with me. (My urologist shared many of the same strategies with me, as well.) If your medical staff approves, I encourage you to follow them.

Drink lots of water. Water helps flush bacteria out of the urinary tract, preventing the harmful microorganisms from staying and multiplying. Bacteria have more of a problem physically holding onto the bladder wall if you drink a lot. Drinking throughout the day is important, and you should never wait until you feel thirsty.

D-Mannose, a sugar found in cranberries, is good for us. It binds itself to *E. coli* and helps to make it harder for the bacteria to attach to the bladder wall[1]. As a result, it works as a first line of defense against *bladder infections* if even a small number of bacteria reach the bladder. Besides eating and drinking anything cranberry, I also buy D-Mannose in powder form at a health-food store and try to have some every day. D-Mannose is also a natural supplement to antibiotics. When I feel a urinary tract infection coming on, I drink some with a huge amount of water.

Use digestive enzymes. Antibiotics indiscriminately kill off any susceptible bacteria they contact, including our normal flora or good bacteria that help us digest our food. So not only is your body fighting a nasty infection, but the antibiotics can deprive you of the ability to digest food completely and take in important nutrients. I try to always add digestive enzymes to my diet if I need to take an antibiotic. Probiotics are live bacteria that we eat, and they're good for our health. By eating probiotic-laced supplements, I am recolonizing my gut with healthy bacteria.

Probiotics that aid digestion are found in yogurt made with live acidophilus cultures. Eating yogurt is such an easy way to help the gut do its job. Probiotics are also found in a number of other delicious foods that are readily available in the supermarket, such as cheeses, sauerkraut, olives, and yogurt. Probiotics are encouraged to multiply even further when we include spices, tea, red wine, berries, apples, and beans in our diet.

Exercise at least four times a week. Not easy for me, but I always feel better when I do.

Besides following these Tip Time tips, each morning I use my bullet blender to get my day started off right by making a smoothie that includes a scoop of veggie protein, yogurt, blueberries, a scoop of D-Mannose, glutamine, a liquid form of B12, and a liquid multivitamin mix. The resultant drink gets me through a busy morning.

I include vitamin B12 because a B12 deficiency can affect the nervous system and, left untreated, can cause permanent nerve damage. Symptoms can include numbness, tingling in the hands and feet, unsteadiness, difficulty walking, confusion, depression, memory loss, dementia, and . . . Neurogenic Bladder.

Tip Time:

Some supplements I take regularly are B-12, vitamin D, and zinc, D-mannose, and probiotics. Both my naturopath and urologist recommend them. Check with your doctor before adding them to your diet.

If there is something I lack, why not get what I need? I refuse to always be on the defensive. I do not want to wait for the other shoe to drop. I try to go on the offensive and take that ball and run as fast as I can. We need good coaches, not team medics. I would rather have someone offer suggestions on how to keep my body as healthy as possible, rather than only prescribe treatments when it's sick.

Sure, I have a Neurogenic Bladder and Bowel – but why do I sometimes feel worse . . . or better? Does it have something to do with whether my diet includes the vitamins and nutrients I need? Why can't I feel like Napoleon did when he met Josephine? We have only one body. So rather than passively stand by while it deteriorates, why not do everything we can through what we eat to make our body as strong and healthy as possible?

Knowledge Nugget:

Recommendations for improving/maintaining healthy bladder function[3]:

Consume an adequate level of fluid per day to maintain a urination-frequency period of every three to four hours.

Moderate/limit your consumption of food and beverages known to irritate the bladder.[4]

Adopt a relaxed position for urination, and allow time to empty the bladder.

Maintain muscle tone with pelvic-floor muscle training and preemptive pelvic-floor contraction (Knack maneuver) to improve and maintain bladder health.

Avoid or control constipation.

Maintain a healthy weight (obesity can lead to compromised bladder function).

Quit smoking or never start.

The Yearly Physical and Other Medical Care

My family practitioner is such an important person on my team. All the records from my specialists go to her. She manages my care, and I have faith she will do a good job. Sometimes I tend to forget that there is more to me than my bladder and that the rest of my body needs to be nurtured, too.

During my yearly physical, I have blood drawn for various tests. The physician listens to my heart, looks in my mouth, and checks my weight and height, blood pressure, and other statistics. She checks over my whole

Advice from a Chemist:

One Saturday I went to a local lecture by myself. Having arrived a little early, I sat up front. Along came this lively woman with a radiant smile, and I was glad when she sat next to me. I liked her instantly. Her gait was halting so I helped her sit and arrange her purse and cane.

Because my neurologist had told me that a third of patients with Neurogenic Bladder and Bowel have Multiple Sclerosis (MS), I wondered, as my new acquaintance struggled to sit down, if I would be like her in a few years. The surrounding hubbub melted away as we began to talk. We just got lost in conversation about each other's story, as two strangers can. I do not know why I said this, but I asked her outright if she had MS and, in the same sentence, told her that I could have it as well because I had a Neurogenic Bladder.

Aren't you glad you weren't the stranger sitting by me?

Our eyes met, and she began to tell me her very interesting story. She was a chemist and raised horses. Yes, she did have MS, but that was not all. When she was first diagnosed, she had been subjected to many medical tests and medications. Because she was a chemist, she understood the toll they could take on her body. But she was so afraid of the impending illness that she did not care. By the time she spoke with me, she felt she had lost the battle. She had cancer in her bones, and there was no hope for recovery.

This chemist cautioned me to always get a second opinion before I took any medications. In her opinion, many of her doctors prescribed drugs without thinking much about the long-term effects the medications could have on her body and well-being. She suggested that I hire a chemist to go over my prescriptions. A trusted pharmacist is also a good option.

body to make sure nothing is developing that needs my attention. My bladder, bowel, and nervous system are not a big part of this appointment.

But there are times when I need to remind my family-practice physician that my body reacts a little differently than that of the "average" patient. I need to advocate for myself. During one routine physical, the doctor felt my ovaries as part of my pelvic exam. As a woman, I need to be aware of the risks of ovarian cancer. The American Cancer Society estimates that, in the United States in 2014, about 21,980 women would receive a new diagnosis of ovarian cancer and that about 14,270 women would die from it.

So as we went through the pelvic exam, I was listening carefully. The conversation with my doctor went like this:

Tip Time:

Your family-practice doctor is the keeper of all of your records. He or she is the gatekeeper and the only doctor you see that views the whole picture. It is important to see this doctor once a year.

Doctor: One of the symptoms of ovarian cancer is constipation.

Me: Well, since I have a Neurogenic Bowel, I am always constipated; my bowel is chronically sluggish.

Doctor: The other symptom is feeling bloated.

Me: Since I am chronically constipated but use stool softeners, the bloated feeling is not foreign to me.

Doctor: Discomfort in the abdomen is another clue.

Me: There are a lot of reasons that I get twinges of pain once in a while. It is just a way of life for me.

My ovaries were tender after the exam, which is another symptom of ovarian cancer. But the topic was dropped, and, quickly, we were onto the next body part. As much as I like my family-practice physician, I felt like my doctor forgot that I had some nonworking parts and did not really understand that my body had its quirks. As I left the appointment, I wondered if I should have persisted and asked how I can know if I may have ovarian cancer, given that the usual symptoms occur as part of my daily experience with Neurogenic Bladder. I discussed the situation with my urologist, and she suggested that I work with her in the ovary department.

My point in all of this is that, no matter how well we get along with our doctors, we need to prepare for our visits with them, because even "normal" issues can be more complicated when combined with the symptoms of any chronic illness.

And I do mean *prepare.* Even with the weeks or months that may pass before I can see a specialist and then the time spent in the waiting room before that appointment, I know from experience that, without preparation, some things will get missed. I may practice what I want to say over and over again, but because of the emotional state I find myself in when I finally get to see the specialist, my mind can go blank. I get tongue-tied and forget important facts I should share. I have so many embarrassing questions having to do with pooping, peeing, sex, and passing gas – topics I *never* talk about with *anyone,* but I have only five to ten minutes to get down and dirty.

What to do? I keep a medical journal. In it is a calendar of all my medical appointments. In the front of it, I also keep a list of my medications, including any herbal supplements and vitamins. When a doctor prescribes a new medication, I write down its exact spelling and what the side effects can be. I have found that the best person to talk to about side effects is a pharmacist.

I also use my medical journal for recording questions I want to ask at my next appointment. When the questions I need to ask make my toes curl with embarrassment, just reading them helps. I realize my doctor can't read my mind. If I am better organized, the doctor has a better chance of giving me what I need: solid advice, empathy, and empowerment. I also include a "shopping list" of medications, such as extra antibiotics, for which I may need new prescriptions. Discussing medications provides a perfect opportunity to ask what other things I can do to help my body be as healthy as possible.

Tip Time:

Discussion points with my doctor might include:

- *My current, past, or recurring symptoms. I record them on the calendar so the doctor can see how often and when they occur. It helps to be really clear. The symptom may seem little or insignificant to me, but to the doctor, it might be a real clue to the cause of my discomfort or affliction.*
- *How long the symptom has been happening.*
- *How uncomfortable the symptom is on a scale from one to ten.*
- *Questions for the doctor such as: Are there new cures or treatments available or ways to eliminate my symptoms? Are there new findings for my condition that can help me? Can you offer me advice for coping that you may have learned from other patients?*

When I'm at my appointment, I refer to the information in my medical journal, and either I or a family member who accompanies me takes notes. (Sometimes I record my notes immediately after the appointment.) My notes include answers to questions, advice, names of tests given, and the results.

Like most people with a chronic illness, I see several doctors. They don't always communicate with each other, so keeping a notebook helps me help them keep things straight. If a test sounds like something another doctor recently administered, I can quickly check in my journal and let the doctor know. I need to be aware and advocate for myself.

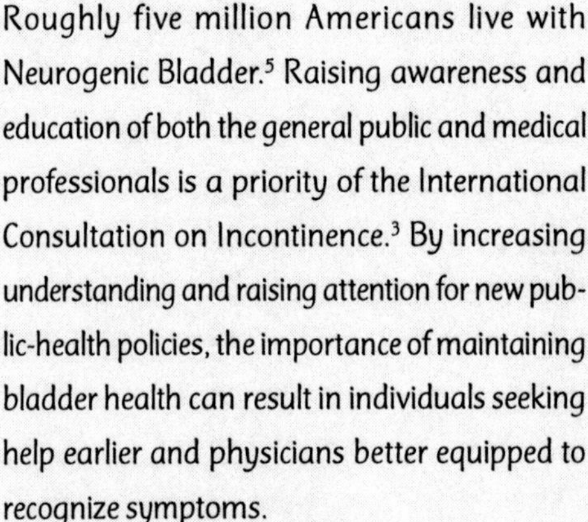

Knowledge Nugget:

Roughly five million Americans live with Neurogenic Bladder.[5] Raising awareness and education of both the general public and medical professionals is a priority of the International Consultation on Incontinence.[3] By increasing understanding and raising attention for new public-health policies, the importance of maintaining bladder health can result in individuals seeking help earlier and physicians better equipped to recognize symptoms.

We need competent and empathetic doctors. To me, empathetic doctors listen and are willing to acknowledge that sometimes life with Neurogenic Bladder is really challenging. I feel comfortable with them, which allows me to raise and discuss difficult subjects. I have no time or patience for a medical professional who has the attitude that I just need to buck up. I put on a brave front for many of my friends and all of my coworkers. At the doctor's office, I want to be able to be real and let it rip – *whatever* I'm currently going through. I expect to receive solid answers to the many questions that I do not have the nerve to ask anyone else, and I need help understanding when those answers are extremely complicated or buried in medical language.

Empathetic doctors make me feel like they are really on my team. This is more than just knowing about my symptoms. It is about understanding me and feeling my embarrassment or shame as things that I have no control over happen to my body. Compassion is critical because, since my disability is private and hidden, few other people are in a position to really understand the challenges I face every day. It is important for me to feel that I am understood, valued, and accepted, especially by someone who is in a position to help me manage my symptoms in the best way possible. I want to be able to identify and partner with my doctors, kind of like being in a club with others who have the same interests. I want doctors who are positive and hopeful.

Obviously, if our medical needs are not met, our health can deteriorate fast and we might face death before we are ready. We all agree on choosing a doctor who is medially competent, but empathy has a practical side and actually increases a doctor's competence. Patients are more than just a bundle of symptoms: they are individuals who are dealing with symptoms, and the doctor's attitude can make so much difference – it can hearten or discourage them, and a patient's state of mind can greatly influence his or her health.

I realize that many people have to wait a very long time to see a specialist, and when they finally get to see one, being picky about the personality of that urologist or neurologist is not an option. I get that. Some patients with Neurogenic Bladder and Bowel get very little empathy from their doctors. Is it because of a lack of time? The subject matter? Is it a right brain vs. left brain issue? For years, I have heard the excuse that the doctor is really good but has no bedside manner. To me, that's not good enough. Empathy is something we all can learn – including doctors.

Let's appreciate the many doctors who are both empathetic and competent, and encourage the medical community to understand our longing to be treated as living souls, not numbers or meal tickets.

Working

My working career has been scattered because my top priority was raising my own children. I have taught at schools. I have volunteered at schools, I have sold jewelry, and currently I am enjoying work in a special-education program at a local high school. The kids I work with keep me on my toes. I love my job because it offers me the chance to work with our country's future – all of our children.

My success at working while having Neurogenic Bladder has depended on accessible toilet facilities. I tried using restrooms closer to my classroom, but that arrangement did not work out for a huge reason: hygiene. The toilet in the nurse's office is perfect because there is a sink in the toilet area; it is essential to wash my hands. In fact, I spend a lot of time washing my hands because I come in contact with so many kids. We share computer keyboards and pencils, plus I sit within sneezing distance.

I keep an extra box of catheters in the nurse's office, which is a lifesaver on days when I completely forget to bring my pouch of supplies with me. I have full privacy there as well, and I'm lucky that I work with a population that can be a bit self-absorbed and not even notice my occasional treks to the nurse's office. I also keep a change of clothes at work. I have not needed them, thank goodness, but they are there, just in case.

Because I have a documented disability, I have rights at work that are stipulated in the government guidelines to protect workers with disabilities[6,7]. That said, because of the personal nature of my disability, I have not made my needs too public. The nurse knows, of course, because she sees me several times a day, as well as the teachers and staff whom I work with directly. So far, that has been adequate. We move in and out of our work day like a well-oiled machine; my colleagues cover for me just as I cover for them, and we all get our jobs done.

My supervisor is not even aware of my exact medical issues, but my emergency card on file includes contact information for both my family doctor and my neurologist.

I get frequent bladder infections, so at times I need to walk all the way to the nurse's room three times a day – much more frequently than when I first started working at the school. So far, I've been able to plan bathroom visits at lunch and between classes. Because it can be easy to get absorbed in work and forget about those necessary trips, I have found it is easy to remind myself by using an alarm clock, timer, or an app for my iPhone that I can set at regular intervals.

Usually I can schedule doctors' appointments after work or in the summer. When I was first diagnosed and was going through many doctors' appointments and testing, I was amazed by what late hours my hospital keeps. I missed only one half-day at work, and I was able to do all the MRIs and other tests after school.

During that crazy time, being with the kids and my workmates at school made my life seem normal. Even now, as the workday progresses and I engage in the lives and learning of the students, I forget my aches and pains and truly enjoy what I am doing.

I had the opportunity to travel to Japan one summer as a chaperone for a group of students from two different high schools. It was such an adventure. I experienced several glitches, however. One weekend, we traveled to the very hot city of Kyoto. The catheters I took melted in the heat. The melting of the catheter was a surprise to me. In any case,

I would have had to go to a hospital to buy what I needed, if I had not taken along some sample catheters that did not melt in the heat. If you are going to an area that is overly scorching, perhaps bringing along several varieties of catheters is a good idea.

Back in school at Osaka, I threw away my used catheters in the restroom trashcan. Living in the States, I always imagined a custodian emptying the trash and gave the contents no thought. In Japan, though, the kids clean their own schools. How novel! They even clean the restrooms. Well, the kids found my catheters. How embarrassing! There was a lesson to be learned. Get those zip-lock bags, carry out the slimy tubes, and dispose of them in a more generic, public trashcan.

I also learned another great lesson: when work is involved, it is advantageous to be up-front about my health limitations. As part of a team, sometimes I need to suck up my pride and not act like I'm Superwoman. Being secretive created stress for me. It also denied others the opportunity to show compassion as well as learn that we are all, indeed, human and do not need to be physically perfect to do a good job in our professional endeavors.

When I look back over my employment, I realize I have been fortunate. Many others do not enjoy their work environment. I have been offered support and alliance. I try to be discreet and professional, understanding that, unfortunately, there are others who have Neurogenic Bladder and Bowel who have far more restrictions than I do.

How much longer will I work? I don't know. For that matter, none of us knows what the future will bring. But we all deserve to experience full and rich lives, whether that involves the workplace or elsewhere. I often remember the saying, "When God closes a door, He opens up windows." We need to look for those windows. While the future may be a mystery, we can count on the present. So let's live!

Traveling

A trip or vacation can be a mixed blessing. It can add stress to my life because I am thrown off schedule, and the location of the next toilet is unpredictable. Yet something happens to my attitude when I pack for a trip. It is so exciting. The anticipation of getting away makes my heart sing.

However, if I do not pack what I need, my life can quickly become miserable. My Costa Rica trip horror happened on a boat: a bowel accident with no toilet paper on board. I went unprepared, and it was miserable. If I had thought to bring an extra change, a zip-lock bag, and wet wipes, I would have been fine. A travel lesson learned: Be prepared!

Sometimes, being prepared is not enough. I was once in New York City, and I went from shop to shop, asking to use a toilet. Even McDonald's would not let me in. Well, you all know how that ended. My fault, indeed. I was too cheap to spend a dollar to buy a drink so I could use the bathroom.

It might be tempting to stay at home, because I know accidents happen. I have lived through several of them. My solace is that I will never see those people again, and, in the meantime, I have made wonderful memories through the rest of my travel. When I am out and about, I don't feel the pain in my bladder. I get to experience something new and the beauty God has to offer.

Based on lessons learned, in packing for a trip, I try to keep a list going of things I need. Even if I don't fly, I like to travel light enough to use a carry-on bag. If I have only a small space for my things, I need to pack smart.[8] I keep extra meds and personal items always packed in a travel case, even at home. Then, when I get ready to leave home for a few days, all is ready. The most important items are devices, meds, and the wow-factor wardrobe to put the spring in my step. I make sure my outfits mix and match so I don't suffer wardrobe meltdowns if something becomes soiled. Bringing a little laundry soap and a Tide Stain Stick helps as well.

Layering is key. It keeps me warm, yet helps me cool down, too. If something becomes unusable, it does not become a problem. I can easily wear another clothing item. Jeans, sweaters, and coats are bulky, so I stay clear of them if I can.

I always take an extra soft bag with a zipper, like a beach bag that can fold up small so it does not take up much room when not in use. I can use it for picnics and carry items that I need on day trips. And I use it to pack gifts for the trip home. It has many uses, and I never leave home without one.

I never pack my catheters or other life-saving items in just one place. I carry some with me in my makeup case and send other items through in checked bags. Whatever I do, I pack enough! There is always a risk that the bag will not arrive when I do, so taking what I need is paramount. I also keep a prescription for catheters on hand. That way, I can get replacements if my catheters are lost, and, in case of a medical emergency, I can easily explain my medical needs.

Tip Time:

I prepack a pill cylinder that holds:

Prilosec and Tums

Bladder pain med

Just-in-case antibiotic

Stool softener and laxative

Advil

Melatonin to help with jet lag

Vitamins, probiotics, and baby aspirin

Within the pouch that I strap around my waist, I carry my wallet, catheters, a wet-wipe product, and extra zip-lock bags. The zip-lock bags are great for packing a lunch, storing soiled clothing items, and containing used catheters. There is another item I have considered including in my pouch: a condom. Yes, you read correctly – a condom. When I use my catheter, I need clean hands. Finding a sink is not always possible. When I insert a catheter, I use my ring finger to guide the catheter into my urethra. That ring finger needs to be really clean. Why not put a sterile condom on the ring finger to prevent germs from entering my bladder?

Traveling in the United States, my cell phone is more than a phone; it is where I keep my emergency phone numbers and calendar and a place to write reminders.

Flying with a Neurogenic Bladder can be a challenge for several reasons. It starts at the airport with security. At times, I carry large syringes filled with an antibiotic solution, along with my catheters. Because I'm concerned about getting the liquid past security, I have a letter from my doctor, which I hope will be sufficient. My biggest fear is that some guy from security will want to manhandle the liquid – even test it. The syringe needs to be clean and sterile. It will go inside my body. One time, a person in security took my catheters out at an airport and, after closely looking at them, said, "What is this for?" I was so shocked and horrified that I simply mumbled something about it being a woman's clean intermittent catheter. The situation took my breath away. It was a little like having the metal detector blaring "beep, beep" after going past my underwire bra in front of God and everybody. Sometimes, going through airport security is just plain hard.

Once onboard, the challenges are not over. Toilets on airplanes are extra short. As I tried to cath on one flight, I was horrified to see the stream of urine from my catheter was going under the toilet seat onto the floor. I mopped up what I could with a paper towel. I have heard of people with Neurogenic Bladders peeing into a plastic bottle, then dumping the urine into the toilet. There is just not a lot of room in the toilet area on airplanes to manage easily.

Whatever you do, don't sit in the front three rows on a long flight. Recently, on a five-hour flight, I had to use the restroom. I was in row 11. Because the cart was servicing the back rows, I needed to stand in line to use the first-class restroom. Four people stood in front of me. Finally I got to the front of the line, but just as I was going to get my turn, they finished serving food and asked us to use the restroom to the rear. After the about-face, all the people behind me were in front of me, and I had to wait again. If you are sitting on the edge of your chair to see how this turned out, I am happy to report all was well. When I returned to my seat, my husband asked, "What is that smell? Not you, is it?" I am happy to report that it was not. But honestly, it could have been, for as long as I had to wait.

Having Neurogenic Bladder and Bowel presents unique challenges, but it does not mean we have to hibernate. By taking proactive steps for our health and well-being and by preparing to handle worst-case scenarios, we can embrace life. Now go take that trip and have an adventure!

9. Parenting a Child with Neurogenic Bladder

Before I had my children, I was so free with my parenting advice. Now I have four children and grandchildren as well, and I am completely at a loss for words and aware of how very little I know.

—JoAnne Lake

As parents, we need to remember that our reactions to the little things in life matter a lot. There are many reasons children can be incontinent. They could be born with Tethered Cord Syndrome or nerve damage to the spinal column that is not noticeable at birth but is very evident at the time of potty training. Or, like my daughter, they could have incontinence for another reason. As a new parent, I did not have a clue what the road ahead would be like for my daughter and me. Many parents are in similar circumstances for all kinds of reasons. Kids come in all sorts of shapes and sizes, and mine was no different.

My daughter Anika has a Neurogenic Bladder, but hers is different from mine. Rather than dealing with Urine Retention because of a flaccid or unresponsive bladder, she has a spastic or overactive bladder and lives with "urge incontinence." When she has to go, sometimes she has to *go.*

All her life, she has had a bladder that would give her very little warning before it emptied. The time between her voiding signal and when she needs to get to the toilet is very short.

Early Days

Our family lived in Salinas, California, while Randy worked at Fort Ord, and we decided to send our three-year-old daughter, Anika, to preschool. She was already reading, and I was eager to get her going with other kids and for her to have the fulfilling experience of friends and teachers. At home, she used our toilet and was somewhat potty trained, so I thought the time was right. She still had some accidents, but not regularly.

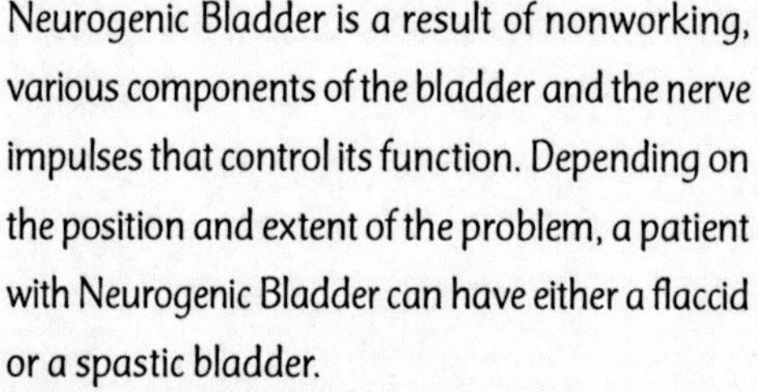

Knowledge Nugget:

Neurogenic Bladder is a result of nonworking, various components of the bladder and the nerve impulses that control its function. Depending on the position and extent of the problem, a patient with Neurogenic Bladder can have either a flaccid or a spastic bladder.

During that first week of school, I was surprised to find myself picking her up early every day because she had wet pants. She seemed to be the only child in this situation, and it caught me off guard. She was my first child and, as I shared my experiences with other mothers, I realized that, although it was normal for preschoolers to have toileting accidents, hers were the most frequent of the group. I supposed that part of the problem was that, at home, I would frequently remind her to use the toilet. At school, she needed to feel the urge and go by herself, without being prompted.

Nevertheless, I was alarmed because, in so many ways, Anika was a social, smart, loving child, and I did not want her bladder to cause her problems with fitting in with the other children and enjoying school. I worried that frequent accidents would jeopardize her being allowed to attend school at all. I could not imagine her being deprived of the opportunity to learn more, but the teachers at the preschool were kind and encouraging. I think I was more concerned than they were.

I held Anika home from preschool several times, because I was humiliated and embarrassed. When I look back, I know I was prideful and bewildered. I did not understand that this would be a chronic condition for my daughter. I had the naïve view that her life could be controlled, that I could change her world through my worry and concern. "Did I sign up for this?" I wondered. I had a lot to learn about parenting and, at that time, having a daughter who had no bladder control made no sense to me.

I read all of the toilet training books. I had M&Ms and stickers for incentive rewards and made a fancy chart to mark her triumphs and encourage her. I talked to the doctor and my friends with small children. I continued to read and read.

Nothing worked. It was what it was. So instead of being a roll-with-the-punches mom, I felt more like I was the punching roll. My pride and my inability to control an uncontrollable situation made me feel like a failure as a mother.

Had I known then what I know now, I would have slapped a diaper on her and not given the situation a moment's thought, but, at the time, I was bewildered. In every other way, she was sharp, cute, and well adjusted. I wanted and longed for order and perfection (remember, I was a young mother), and this ongoing, unpredictable situation did not fit well in my cookie-cutter, trying-to-be-well-ordered life. How could my daughter forget to use the restroom?

When I look back over this period of our life, I think I did my best, but I had some weepy, angry, frustrated moments. It was hard trying to run out the door, and, at the last minute, face my daughter's need for a complete outfit change. I tried to be a loving, nurturing mother, but, at times, I would blow my cork, because we were running late for an appointment or because a situation was completely out of my control.

As the years passed, I got over my frustrations. We learned to build in time for the extra change of clothes or brought an extra set of clothes in the car with us, just in case it was needed. We still encountered accidents, but I adjusted, and we did what had to be done. If Anika had had a different personality type, the potential social stigma might have brought her down, and things could have been much worse. It never stopped her, though.

Elementary School Years

We moved to the Seattle area and enrolled Anika in kindergarten. As she moved through elementary school, she was able to hide her problem herself by tying her sweater around her waist. I sent her to school wearing sanitary pads. After a pad became soaked with urine, she left it in the bathroom trash. Her friends at school never noticed or perhaps just did not care. The staff at the school knew a little of what we dealt with, because, at times, we needed to bring in a clothing change for her, but no one made a big deal about it. She attended a small, private school, so there was no school nurse. Regardless, she learned to cope, taking it in stride with little trauma or embarrassment. It was the only life she'd ever known and normal for her.

Anika also had chronic bladder infections as a child. Finally, we were referred to the Children's Orthopedic Hospital in Seattle, which at the time housed the Pediatric Urology Clinic. Her doctor prescribed low-dose antibiotics. She took Ditropan for many years. During our visits, she was slimed with gel in preparation for an ultrasonic peek at her kidneys and continually underwent panels of urodynamic tests. The doctors told us that, once she reached puberty, she would outgrow her incontinence and chronic bladder infections because her urethra would elongate. The term *Neurogenic Bladder* was never mentioned. I did not hear the term until I myself was diagnosed many years later.

I don't remember a nurse pulling me aside to give me tips on how I could help my daughter. The doctors were concerned for her medically but did not address the logistics of keeping her dry or coping with accidents, so we came up with our own solutions.

As Anika got older, I no longer had the urge to divulge her private life to other mothers – well, mostly. I have always enjoyed talking about my children, and Anika had so many attributes to be proud of: she was an excellent student, an outstanding athlete, and an expert equestrian. As time went on, I became less focused on her bladder-control problems because she was taking care of them herself. Instead I was enjoying her accomplishments.

During her elementary school years, she was a busy child who ran like the wind and came home dirty from play. She was a rough-and-tumble kid and was more interested in having a good time than worrying about hygiene. Honestly, not once did she ever complain. She was ready to live her life, and she knew, even though I did not, that this life was normal for her. She just wanted to move on and enjoy it.

I still worried that she would be caught. Her situation was a safely guarded secret in our family. At times, I was annoyed at the inconvenience and was even a bit put out because of this uncontrollable bladder of hers. I did not know the medical name. I just knew it was a condition that was talked about in hushed tones and whispers for fear of embarrassing my daughter – or myself, if I was completely honest.

Changes

Anika entered junior high, and, just as the doctors had predicted, her chronic wetting problem ceased. Her urethra elongated with puberty, and she outgrew her painful bladder infections as well. She stopped her regular appointments at the urology clinic, although she did have an occasional accident. She still does.

Today Anika has to pay attention to where the toilet is because she does not have much time to get there, due to a spastic bladder. She also learned in college not to drink a lot of alcohol because it made her wet the bed.

Tip Time:

Diet and drink options affect the severity of symptoms experienced by patients with Incontinence/ Neurogenic Bladder. Be conscious and knowledgeable about which choices affect you.

The rest of the story...

After talking with her doctor and doing some research on her own, Anika decided, before the birth of her first children, to find a doctor who would give her a cesarean section, because she did not want to jeopardize or compromise her bladder further. She and her loving husband are the proud parents of twin daughters. She is currently not taking meds and is not seeing a urologist. She simply copes with a bladder that needs attention and can't be ignored. She recognizes her warning signs.

Giving Our Children What They Need

People who do not live with incontinence often think that life with diapers, cathing, occasional accidents, and the rest of it is a death sentence. These feelings are magnified if they learn one of their children will be living with incontinence. But it is not a death sentence. For those of us who deal with these issues, they are part of our normal lives.

We need to treat our children who have bladder issues as normal and take the drama, pain, sorrow, and anguish out of the equation as much as possible. These children deserve to be thought of as normal, because they are. This is how their bodies work. We don't have many cures for nerve damage yet, so this life is what our children will know.

Knowledge Nugget:

Patients with Spastic Bladder may experience irregular urination frequency, Nocturia (or bed wetting) and/or Urgency Incontinence (or Spastic Paralysis) due to sensory nerve deficits. Their bladders can contract without warning, releasing urine.

Knowledge Nugget:

Psychological experiences can impact our biological systems. A panel of experts studying bladder health recognized that the health of the adult bladder can be impacted by incidents from childhood, including access *frequency* to bathroom facilities.[1] The panel's goal is that, by improving the understanding of normal toileting patterns and the effect of interruption by "environmental factors," we can avert situations in which toilets become the scenes of bullying and lead to unhealthy "holding behavior."[2] It is the act of holding and not voiding that can subsequently lead to damage to the bladder over time. Securing bathroom privacy, safety, and cleanliness for children and adults in schools should be a given and can be achieved through proactive work on the part of parents, educators, and administrators.

If you are sharing your life with a sweet child who chronically loses control of her bladder, I completely understand feelings of sorrow, frustration, pride, and even anger that go along with your situation. Emotions are a real part of life, and sometimes we need to simply face up to them. It is hard as a parent to watch a child we love so much suffer. So we try to shield her to prevent any pain or ridicule that may be heading her way. Of course, no parents can completely control their children's circumstances. And most children will be bothered to one degree or another by teasing from other children. Our children have to learn how to live with the challenges of life.

When I look back at how sometimes I reacted to Anika when she was a little girl, I wish I had done things differently. I was impatient at times, but the most heartbreaking memories for me involve my complete lack of understanding of the chronic condition that my daughter had. I did not understand that wetting her pants was normal for her, so, at times, I was surprised or taken off guard by an accident and then felt frustrated.

The other mistake I made during those years is that I did not ask doctors and other professionals about strategies for coping with day-to-day circumstances. I could also have sought out a support group with other parents where we could share our coping techniques.

Luckily I did not cause Anika to be ashamed of herself because of my own shame. Once I understood the situation better, we all just did what we needed to do to encourage and support her.

If I could relive this part of my life again, the embarrassment I felt and the fear of others' finding out would not be part of the equation. Today I understand that Neurogenic Bladder is a medical condition that affects many kids and adults alike. It is just an ailment that many do not talk about, and, unfortunately, because of the lack of discussion, many parents feel isolated, as I did. My hope is that you won't make the same mistakes that I did.

Of course, sympathy for our children has its place; I get that. If our children are sad, worried, and upset, then, by all means, we should show that we hear their pain and want to be there for them. Mirroring or acknowledging their emotions is so appropriate because it tells them that they are being heard and understood.

However, it is important for us to realize that sympathy is not always helpful. When a person of any age is living with a chronic physical issue and the situation will never change or go away, it feels more like a job – especially after the initial adjustment to the new normal. Imagine yourself working at a hard, painful job, and your boss comes up to you and says, "I am so sorry you have to do this job. My heart bleeds for you. This is so incredibly difficult." Would such negative, depressing words inspire you to keep trying? Couldn't you do your job better if your boss praised you for your great effort and a job well done?

Just so, our children need to be encouraged as they struggle to adjust to their lives. If we see our children working hard to cope with the situation life has dealt them, we should offer a compliment because it is a job well done. The child with Neurogenic Bladder needs a cheerleader, someone who says, "You can do this!" "I am proud of you." "You are working hard, and I think that you are amazing because you do the job so well."

Undeniably, when our children are having a particularly hard day, they need our empathy. But, if the child is coping the way a lot of kids do, wanting to change out of the soiled clothes fast so he can go out to play, we're of more help by assisting in that goal without inserting a bunch of questions and sympathetic expressions that he really is not interested in. While it may be heartbreaking for us to watch our children go through challenging times, we need to guard against drowning them in sympathy and sorrow when they don't need it. When our kids are doing their best to cope and just want to be treated normally, they don't need our drama. Praise is so much more powerful and, of course, if needed, that helping hand to get out the door to the next activity.

Sometimes, as parents, we seem to think everything that happens to our children is all about us: our convenience, what kind of parents we look like to others, whether or not we are good parents. For example, when there's an accident, we may find ourselves embarrassed that we're going to be late to an appointment *again*. How will this make us look to the doctor's staff? In anger and frustration, we tell our child, "If you'd paid better attention, you would not have caused us to be late again." In retrospect, we recognize the situation could have been handled differently and feel overwhelmed by guilt. What did we do wrong? What can we change? For me, I needed to learn to take a step back and look at the situation from Anika's perspective. An accident could be just that: an accident caused by her lack of bladder control – not a consequence of laziness or an indictment of my parenting skills.

Children want to please their parents, so when we transfer our problems and emotions onto them, blaming them for how we feel, it's hard on everybody. Sometimes the problems we deal with as parents are bigger than what we can handle on our own. Many parents benefit by finding a friend or counselor on whom they can unload their sorrows. These people can help us gain much-needed perspective.

Motherhood can be complicated. I have found it to be empowering, prideful, frustrating, and the loveliest experience of my life. When I first became a mother and accepted the responsibility for another's life and well-being, my own childhood was pushed aside, and, at times, I was in over my head. Probably most young mothers are a bit overwhelmed. Everything is so new.

When, three years later, I began dealing with my daughter's Neurogenic Bladder, I did not feel comfortable finding help for us. I was afraid that calling attention to the situation would cause more problems than it would solve. I kept so much to myself.

Since then, our society has become more open about many medical conditions, but one could argue that chronic issues with bladder and bowel control are still somewhat hidden from view. My hope is that those of us with children who have Neurogenic Bladder will no longer let our own or society's embarrassment keep us in isolation, walking alone in the shadows, fearful of what may happen if our secret is discovered. May we walk forward in freedom, uniting with medical professionals and other parents to create a world for our children where Neurogenic Bladder is an accepted part of their lives but not the definition of who they are.

10. Not Broken, but Beautiful: Moving Beyond Embarrassment

The little red reed, bending to the force of the wind,
soon stood upright again when the storm passed over.

—Aesop

This book is meant to be a friend for you: a companion guide to encourage you to get out and live your life. I have learned so much on this journey – from the abundance of highs to the many lows. We are not alone. We are a club, of sorts, that holds a common secret. If you are able to take anything away from my writing and musings, please make it this: you are not alone!

If you feel isolated, I want you to consider the woman in the crowd . . . a woman described in the Bible, a book that has been a major influence in history, laws and literature. As long as women have had babies and endured rape and other forms of trauma to their urogenital tracts,[12] some women have been broken and become social outcasts. Here's how the Bible describes one such woman:

25 And a certain woman, which had an issue of blood twelve years,

26 And had suffered many things of many physicians, and had spent
all that she had, and was nothing bettered, but rather grew worse,

27 When she had heard of Jesus, came in the press behind, and touched his garment.

28 For she said, If I may touch but his clothes, I shall be whole.

29 And straightway the fountain of her blood was dried up; and she felt in her body that she was healed of that plague.

30 And Jesus, immediately knowing in himself that virtue had gone out of him, turned him about in the press, and said, Who touched my clothes?

31 And his disciples said unto him, Thou seest the multitude thronging thee, and sayest thou, Who touched me?

32 And he looked round about to see her that had done this thing.

33 But the woman fearing and trembling, knowing what was done in her, came and fell down before him, and told him all the truth.

34 And he said unto her, Daughter, thy faith hath made thee whole; go in peace, and be whole of thy plague.

—Mark 5:25-34

For twelve years, this woman had tried repeatedly to find help and healing. We don't know exactly what was wrong with her, other than that it involved hemorrhaging, but many of us can relate to what she experienced. Nothing seemed to help. Money was spent with little, if any, positive results. Her condition seemed to be getting worse. In her society, a woman who was bleeding in this way was ostracized, an outcast, avoided because she was unclean.

Rather than giving up, she persisted in seeking help. When she heard about Jesus and the miracles he had performed, she left her home to seek him out, risking public rejection and humiliation. The story tells how Jesus publicly recognized her faith and healed her.

Whatever the particulars of our situation, it is important to follow the example of the woman in the crowd. We need to look for solutions. The diagnosis of Neurogenic Bladder and Bowel is not a passive situation. If we are not proactive about our health and daily lives, our existence can become dire. Our world is meant to be filled with obstacles. We can count on them. Watching others, I am sure we can come up with many examples of taking a negative situation and making it work. Let me tell you a story about my dad . . . .

Tip Time From the Woman in the Crowd:

Reach out for help.

Do not stay home and brood.

Be brave and bold.

Take a chance.

A Father's Example

My father retired after a fine agricultural career with Mann Packing Company in the Salinas Valley of California. He was always looking for ways to turn problems into possibilities. One of his ideas was to put cut vegetables on the market, a practice that became an extremely lucrative business for the Salinas Valley.

While he was working for Mann, my dad heard George H. W. Bush on the network news one night saying that he hated broccoli and would never allow broccoli on Air Force One. When you work for a large agricultural concern, negative publicity about any vegetable is a big problem. But President Bush's words got my dad's creative juices going. By the end of the week, he had angry Salinas broccoli farmers going to Washington DC to dump their greens on the White House lawn.

The radio and TV hype about the broccoli caravan was a sensation, and, by the time the truckloads of broccoli had reached our nation's capital, my dad had arranged for a broccoli boutonniere to go to the White House and truckloads of that "green gold" to go to DC soup kitchens. That advertisement stunt not only put Salinas's broccoli on the map, it also made the senior President Bush forever be associated with broccoli.

I smile when I remember this story because my father turned a situation that could have been simply more bad publicity for broccoli into a boost for the agricultural business. That principle of turning a problem into a solution helped me persist in finding the help and support I needed once I was diagnosed with Neurogenic Bladder and Bowel.

Support Groups

I was looking for a solution, or at least a way to put a positive spin on a on a not-so-positive situation, so, like my father did with the negative publicity on broccoli, I needed to find others to help me. He used the media to stir up the hype to help others understand that broccoli is great. I needed to find others to help me find key living answers as well. Since we do not live in a vacuum, the human element is so very important. I needed to find my herd, my group, and my kindred spirits.

Find a support group that fits you. Reaching out is good for our emotional health. The right support group will allow you to get graphic and real, and share your innermost thoughts. Needing to express ourselves and connect is the joy of living. My contact on line with others who have the same condition I do has helped me immensely. They offer me help, encouragement, and assistance in finding new techniques and products. Even though many are untrained medical professionals that does not matter to me because they are very knowledgeable in what I need to know. They deal with the same daily issues I do, they share techniques, products, and loving support, and offer acceptance. They reinforce me and are a pillar of strength. Understanding me, they are like a mirror that helps me better understand myself.

I can talk about topics that might make other friends cringe. People affected with Neurogenic Bladder and Bowel often keep that part of their lives secret from their casual acquaintances and even closer friends, not necessarily because we want to, but because it's clear our friends don't want to know any details. Who wants that kind of information anyway? Most people unaffected by bladder and bowel problems don't want to know. Being selective about your audience is important. After a while, it is possible to get almost too comfortable talking about our bladder and bowel issues because we live with them every day.

There is no "shock effect" with a support group, because they know exactly what I am talking about. They empathize and are familiar with my daily routine. Online, I have chatted about absorbent products, Botox injections for treatment of bladder incontinence, bladder cancer, the color of urine, and all kinds of topics that others have no interest in, yet for me, at a particular time, the pressing need to know is paramount.

The simplest way to find a group is to put "Neurogenic Bladder, Bowel" in a search engine and browse the listings; several groups and forums pop up within the top hits. Several websites have provided me a voice. I am a member of an online bladder and kidney support group, and several Facebook groups. I have found them to be places where we can let it all hang out; there is no fear of making someone uncomfortable. They provide a place where I can voice my ideas and concerns with people who have similar symptoms and problems.

I have gotten loads of really helpful information and leads on all kinds of products from online support groups. I think you will discover there is a wealth of information and support to be had that will help you make some of the tough decisions, plus provide a real place to vent.

Beauty from Adversity

I collect sea glass – pieces of clear and colored glass that were, at some point, thrown into the ocean, broken, and are now polished and made beautiful from years of being tossed in the waves and scoured on the sand. The excitement is in the hunt as I walk along the beach, enjoying the water and waves. Imagine: what was once garbage has become a treasure beyond measure.

On my birthday one year, my adult daughters whisked me off to an island near our home to look for sea glass and enjoy some wine tasting. Throughout the day, I marveled at how God could work in my life. I actually survived bringing up two wildly outrageous and difficult daughters and have lived long enough to see the other side. They planned such a perfect day.

As I walked on the beach with my daughters that day, I glanced down. Right between my toes sat a cobalt blue pebble. Happy Birthday! Thank you! That made my birthday just the best.

If a bottle floats on the sea and never encounters a storm or smashes into some other debris, it may come to rest on the sand and eventually be buried forever. But if it hits rough seas and crashes on the rocks, it will break. The resultant fragments will be tossed about and eventually burnished into the treasured pieces of sea glass that I collect.

Are not our setbacks a bit like sea glass? As we encounter adversity, we are forced to adapt and grow. I encourage you to find what works for you – everyone is different and lives with his or her own unique circumstances. I have shared my story with you from the first symptoms to diagnosis, from early strategies to the routines and processes that have helped me live with my new normal. My hope is that reading about my journey may help you discover your own path. As you travel through rough patches, may you be encouraged by the knowledge that others share your struggles and are living their lives in the best way possible.

The last time I was in my urologist's office, I saw a sign that read, "I laughed so hard the tears ran down my leg." I feel good about being in a secret society that feels comfortable with that humor, a world where I can be accepted as I am. I am so very grateful.

Best wishes, dear sisters (and brothers). We have suffered in silence for a long time, just like the woman in the crowd. She inspires me because she reached out to the only person who could possibly help her. She did not remain at home brooding. She took a chance and decided to make a change in her life. Following her example, we can be brave, too.

Just like my dad, I can try to think out of the box a bit. Every answer is not immediately clear or black-and-white. Every solution does not come from a prescription pad. The explanation does not evolve from my completely understanding why I even have a Neurogenic Bladder and Bowel in the first place. I will probably never know why. It is just the way it is. I understand the solution can happen even though the question is still a mystery. I do not want the "why" to be my stumbling block. I need to move on and put purpose in my step.

It is time for us to stand up and say, "Yes, we have this disability, but it does not define who I am." We need to accept that health is only one element of a fulfilling existence and that a Neurogenic Bladder is only a part of the larger journey.

We need to focus on what we can do rather than become defined by what we can't. Together we need to learn to ask questions and seek answers about our own health. And finally, as we all cope with day-to-day situations, we need to stand proud. We can reclaim our lives, step out, and greet that which drives our passions.

My Sincere Wish for You:

Comfort on difficult days,
Smiles when sadness intrudes,
Rainbows to follow the clouds,
Laughter to kiss your lips,
Sunsets to warm your heart,
Hugs when spirits sag,
Beauty for your eyes to see,
Friendships to brighten your being,
Faith so that you can believe,
Confidence for when you doubt,
Courage to know yourself,
Patience to accept the truth,
Love to complete your life.

—Anonymous[4]

Part 2

Blog Chatter

1. "Dear Biosleuth" – Questions Posed by Patients and their Families

The blog www.TrudyTriumph.com provides readers a chance to ask questions and/or share how they feel. What follows are excerpts from the blog, stimulated by that interaction with readers. The questions are answered by Julia Parker, the Biosleuth, who is a researcher by education and training – initially within a research lab, and later as a reference librarian. If the information is out there, she will do her best to find it and honestly report back the facts, summarizing the latest research findings.

Here are some interesting questions we have received . . . and Biosleuth Julia's answers.

I. Dear Biosleuth,

What causes a Neurogenic Bladder?

After receiving a diagnosis of Neurogenic Bladder, it is only reasonable to begin to wonder how this possibly could have happened. A doctor may speak of the "etiology" of the disease, or the causes of your Neurogenic Bladder. There are so many things that happen through life that could contribute to the loss of neurological control of your bladder. This section will explore several of the more common causes that are found in the medical literature.

The goal of discovering how you may have developed a Neurogenic Bladder is not primarily to attribute the loss of your bladder control or pin the blame on any particular event in your life. Rather, this section is to help you better understand if the development of your Neurogenic Bladder is just one symptom of a potentially more deeply rooted medical problem that is surfacing. Other than aging and trauma, most of the other sources discussed in this section that lead to a Neurogenic Bladder result in a gradual loss of complete control of the bladder, through involvement of muscle control, nerves, etc. It is important to think in terms of the big picture or, rather, your body as a whole, if you are diagnosed with a Neurogenic Bladder. Be alert to any hints your body may be trying to tell you about underlying conditions.

What follows is a list of the many pathways that lead to a Neurogenic Bladder. This is by no means a comprehensive listing and, over time, new conditions may be recognized that also lead to a Neurogenic Bladder. For the sake of simplicity and to facilitate our discussion, the various health conditions that can lead to Neurogenic Bladder have been sorted under a single medical heading, although many could have been grouped under multiple headings. For instance, several conditions contain both a genetic component and, once developed, become chronic, but these have been grouped under "Hereditary." The fact that so many disparate paths can lead to or contribute to the development of a Neurogenic Bladder helps illustrate a few overarching concepts to consider:

I. It is difficult to recognize and diagnose a Neurogenic Bladder.

II. Multiple factors can contribute to the development of a Neurogenic Bladder. The origin and development of a Neurogenic Bladder should not be assumed to be an isolated circumstance; it could be a symptom of another serious health problem.

III. Some of these factors could result from bladder dysfunction. You may find yourself facing the age-old quandary, "Which came first: the chicken or the egg?"

IV. Research into the relationship between many diseases and their effect on the bladder is still in its infancy.

Risk Factors for the Development of a Neurogenic Bladder, Grouped Into Eight Health Area Headings:

Health Area Category	Risk Factors Associated with Neurogenic Bladder
AGING	Kidney Stones Pelvic Organ Prolapse Post-Menopausal Changes to the Vagina Erectile Dysfunction (Men) Prostate Enlargement (Men)
CANCER	Bladder Carcinoma Central Nervous System Tumors Human Papillomavirus-induced Cancer Urothelial Carcinoma (Transitional Cell Carcinoma (TCC))
CHRONIC HEALTH CONDITION	Ankylosing Spondylitis (AS) Chronic Inflammation of the Urinary Tract (Interstitial Cystitis or Cystitides) Congestive Heart Failure Severe Constipation Crohn's/Colitis

Diabetes Mellitus (Diabetic Neuropathy/
Dysautonomia)
Lupus
Osteoarthritis
Paget's Disease
Paresis

HEREDITARY

Behçet's Disease
Marfan Syndrome
MTHFR Gene Mutation (Methyl-Tetrahydrofolate
Reductase)
Spastic Paraplegia (Hereditary)
Spina Bifida
Tethered Cord Syndrome
Visceral Neuropathy (Familial)
Wolfram Syndrome

INFECTIOUS DISEASE

Encephalitis
Guillain-Barré syndrome (GBS)
High Fever Resulting in Delirium
HTLV 1&2
Lyme Disease
Meningomyelitis
Polio
Schistosomiasis (Bilharziasis)
Spinal Epidural Abscess
Syphilis
Tuberculosis (chronic);
Ureases (bacterial)
Urinary Tract Infections (chronic)

NEUROLOGICAL DISEASE OR BRAIN-CHEMICAL IMBALANCE	ADHD
	Alcoholism or Chronic Drug Abuse
	ALS
	Alzheimer's Disease
	Anxiety/Depression
	Dementia
	Inflammatory Demyelinating Polyneuropathy (chronic)
	Multiple Sclerosis
	Neural Lesion
	Neurosarcoidosis
	Parkinson's Disease
	Stroke
SUBSTANCE ABUSE/ VITAMIN DEFICIENCY/ DRUG EFFECT	Vitamin D (Kidney)
	Drugs or Alcohol
	Heavy Metal Poisoning
	Overeating
	Prescription Medications
	Smoking
TRAUMA	Accidental Injury to the
	Brain and/or Spinal Column (SPI)
	Cauda Equina Syndrome
	Cerebral Palsy
	Colon Surgery
	Fistula
	Herniated Disks
	High Impact Exercise
	Postpartum Surgical Procedures
	Rape
	Spinal Cord Trauma
	Traumatic Brain Injury (TBI)
	Vaginal Delivery

Effects of Aging: Physiological Changes to Lower Urinary Tract System Can Affect Urination

The Manack study[1] found the mean age of the patients with Neurogenic Bladder to be 62 years, which would put the average patient with Neurogenic Bladder in a postmenopausal state. Postmenopausal changes to the vagina are the result of the absence or near-absence of estrogen in the female body. As the levels of estrogen naturally decrease in the postmenopausal woman, this can lead to structural atrophy of the urogenital passages. Problems such as vaginal dryness, and infectious and noninfectious disorders in the vagina become more common in elderly women[2]. Studies have looked at the effects of replacing the missing hormones to combat these issues. Vaginal estrogen therapy (ET) preparations have been shown to be as effective as systemic oral dosing[3], and, rather than increase the levels of estrogen circulating in the blood, are delivered directly to the problem area. The presence of the hormone at low levels alleviates urogenital symptoms, without affecting endometrial growth. Small increased levels of estrogen result in an increased blood flow around the bladder neck and midurethra. Patients using hormonal cream noticed improvement of their symptoms of stress incontinence and overactive bladder in a clinical trial of hysterectomized postmenopausal women[3].

Furthermore, hormonal cream has been shown to significantly decrease the incidence of both urinary frequency and nocturia, after three months of use. It may be a treatment to consider when talking to your urologist, if you are postmenopausal.

Cancer:

Bladder carcinoma	Central nervous system tumors	Urothelial carcinoma	Squamous cell carcinomas	HPV-infection combined with Long-term Catheterization

Urothelial carcinoma (Transitional cell carcinoma (TCC) is the most common type of bladder cancer. It arises from uncontrolled growth of the tissue on the inner lining of the hollow organs (epithelium) of the bladder and its connecting tubes, which is also known as transitional epithelium.

Squamous cell carcinomas of the urinary bladder are rare in the Western world, where persistent parasitic infections are not a constant health risk. However, you should be aware that both the practice of long-term catheterization, which is used in the treatment of Neurogenic Bladder, combined with human papillomavirus infection (HPV) puts a person at increased risk of developing carcinoma of the urinary bladder. HPV refers to a group of sexually transmitted virus types, rather than a single organism. It is important to be tested for HPV and to consider getting the vaccine, a series of three injections, which has been available since 2006. Vaccination has been shown to prevent disease for any of the types that are not already present in the urogenital tract. A regular pap smear is important to monitor for cervical cancer, which is common in those infected with certain strains of the virus. A 2012 Sloan-Kettering study[4] was the first to report urothelial carcinoma arising in individuals with both Neurogenic Bladder and HPV infection. Diligent monitoring of your evolving health status is important, so visit your care providers, regularly.

Chronic Health Conditions:

Diabetes mellitus, a metabolic disorder caused by a deficiency of insulin, is a debilitating and costly disease with multiple serious complications. Diabetic bladder dysfunction is the clinical name for one of the most common complications of diabetes mellitus, occurring in the lower urinary tract. Diabetic patients who develop bladder dysfunction complain of voiding problems characterized by poor emptying and overflow incontinence or urge incontinence[5]. In other words, control over urination is compromised.

The very nature of Neurogenic Bladder disease is chronic. It can be combined with pain upon urination, especially prior to diagnosis, when bladder pressures are unmonitored, as was the case for JoAnne, and/or if the bladder is inflamed. If the immune system is taking an active part and causing chronic inflammation of the bladder, the cells that line the bladder will be ultrasensitive and possibly unable to perform normal function. A 2010 study looked for changes in the level of a specific protein (urinary nerve growth factor) in patients with bladder disease. Researchers found increased nerve growth factor (NGF)[6] in both Neurogenic Overactive Bladder (NOAB) and Interstitial Cystitis patients. Further study of the pathology of urologic diseases will not only improve medical understanding but determine whether nerve growth factor, for instance, could be used as a diagnostic or prognostic marker for bladder dysfunction, which could revolutionize the field.

Hereditary:

Many genetic conditions or syndromes can lead to issues of bladder control, since they affect multiple systems in the body. For instance, although **Marfan syndrome** is a rare disease of the connective tissue, most commonly associated with unusual length of limbs/height, it is a disease of highly variable symptoms. It is known to cause widening of the sac that surrounds the spinal column in the lower back, resulting in headaches, back pain, or bowel and bladder problems[7] Carl, a Marfan syndrome patient[8] who struggles with Neurogenic Bladder, is just one personal account posted on the Simon Foundation website.

Wolfram Syndrome, extremely rare – worldwide, affects an estimated one in five hundred thousand people[9]. Sixty to 90 percent of people with Wolfram syndrome have a urinary tract problem that might result in Urine Retention. An abnormality in the pituitary gland disrupts the release of the vasopressin hormone, interrupting the regulation of water balance in the tissues and urine production. Eventually, urinary tract problems include obstruction of the ducts between the kidneys and bladder (ureters), a large bladder that cannot empty normally (high-capacity atonal bladder), disrupted urination (due to a nonresponsive bladder sphincter muscle), and sometimes, incontinence.

Abnormalities of the ureters represent a complex and often-confusing subset of urological anomalies that result in numerous symptoms. Current imaging techniques such as fetal ultrasonography[10] can diagnose hydronephrosis, due to an abnormality of the ureters. Ureteral duplication (having an extra ureter or extra ureteral tissue) is the most common renal abnormality in infants, occurring in approximately 1 percent of the population and 10 percent of children who are diagnosed with urinary tract infections[11]. However, incomplete ureteral duplication, in which one common ureter enters the bladder, rarely causes clinical disease. But, the existence of complete ureteral duplication, in which two ureters enter the same side of the bladder (ipsilateral entry), has a higher chance of leading to the change of urine flow backward into the lower ureter resulting in obstruction of the "upper pole" – the other ureter. These conditions can lead to kidney damage, since the internal pressure within the kidneys can increase, damaging the fragile tissue.

Infectious Disease Origin:

A systematic, controlled study of patients with Lyme disease was published in 2013. The results confirm the association of Lyme disease[12] and urinary bladder dysfunction (of the detrusor/bladder muscle itself). Although the study included only a small patient population, results were statistically significant: 35 percent experienced bladder disease.

Meningomyelitis is the result of a wide range of infectious agents including Mumps, Herpes, HIV, HTLV-1, Syphilis[13], Tuberculosis, and Nematodes (Viral, Bacterial, or Parasitic Infectious Agents). These organisms attack the nervous system. The infection is characterized by a slowly progressive weakness and paresthesia of the lower extremities. Eventually, if allowed to progress, bowel and bladder incontinence and paraplegia are the usual outcome.

Neurological Disease, Cognitive Function & Brain-chemical Imbalances:

Progressively debilitating, degenerative, neurological diseases are probably the easiest to grasp as potential causes for a neurological component of the loss of bladder control. Manack, et al.[1] found that Multiple Sclerosis was a coexisting disease in 17.2 percent of patients with Neurogenic Bladder. That means that approximately one in every 5.8 people with Neurogenic Bladder may be living with Multiple Sclerosis. Neural lesions (central or peripheral nerves), which are frequently irreversible, are often the cause of Neurogenic Bladder. In Parkinson's disease (PD), hyperactivity of the bladder/detrusor muscle is the leading cause of urinary dysfunction. However, a 2013 Brazilian study[14] concluded that incontinence is more likely the result of cognitive and psychological factors of living with Parkinson's, rather than worsening motor function, for these patients.

Toxins/Substance Abuse/Vitamin Deficiency/Drug Side Effect:

Vitamin deficiencies can have far-reaching consequences, especially in combination with certain genetic profiles. Could the long-term exposure to toxins generated by the body's daily functions lead to degeneration of organ function or make them more susceptible to the possibility of infection, kidney disease, or cancer?

Toxins can have a drastic effect on the bladder. Exposure to heavy metals may cause a variety of central, peripheral, or autonomic-nervous-system injuries. Heavy metals such as arsenic can be found in drinking water and are known to cause many cancers, including bladder cancer.[15] Cigarette smoking is known to generate more than forty-five known or suspected chemical carcinogens that can lead to numerous health problems, including bladder cancer.[16] Studies have shown that urine leakage is more severe and frequent in smokers[17] vs. nonsmokers.

Knowledge Nugget:

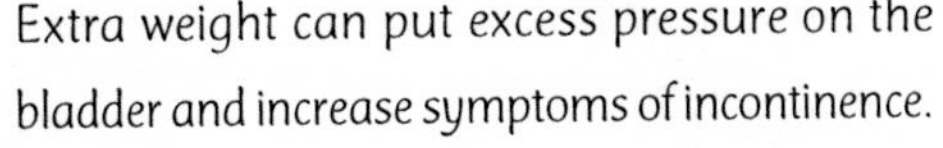
Extra weight can put excess pressure on the bladder and increase symptoms of incontinence.

Trauma — Surgical or Physical Injury:

Sustaining a spinal injury can naturally affect bladder function since the nerves connecting the brain and the bladder may be severed or interrupted. But most women who have a surgical procedure or who experience childbirth do not have any expectation of resulting bladder problems. A "routine" hysterectomy is the most likely primary trigger to the ultimate development of JoAnne's Neurogenic Bladder.

A study of women who had delivered vaginally[17], published in 2012, found that a forceps-assisted delivery increased the odds of each pelvic-floor disorder considered, especially Overactive Bladder (OAB). Of 449 participants, 71 (16%) had Stress Incontinence, 45 (10%) had Overactive Bladder, 56 (12%) had Anal Incontinence, 19 (4%) had Prolapse Symptoms, and 64 (14%) had Prolapse to or beyond the hymen upon examination. Interestingly, the episiotomy procedure, although examined, was not associated with any of these pelvic-floor disorders.

The French urologist Emmanuel Chartier-Kastler, in his 2007 review article[18], concludes how difficult it is to prove the neuro-urological origin of a voiding disorder, whether the result is pelvic pain or post-operative functional disorders, especially following surgical procedures to correct Stress Urinary Incontinence (pelvic repair surgery). The most frequently encountered problem following surgery is Acute Urinary Retention. Surgeons

Knowledge Nugget:

A lot of this section of causes reflects a Neurogenic Overactive Bladder retrospective study[19] of an insurance claims database, "MarketScan" (2002–2006 Claims, Encounters and Medicare Supplemental and Coordination of Benefits), the following conditions of the large insured-patient[1] population were found to coexist with Neurogenic Bladder.

NOTE: Database included ~30 employers for 18–29.2 million patients and Medicare and Medicare supplemental for patients 65 years and over.

can best prevent Acute Urinary Retention by proactively assessing risk factors preoperatively. In addition, Urine Retention can even result once normal urination is resumed, following the removal of the patient's indwelling catheter.

Long-term follow-up to monitor for the possibility of an obstruction (which must be removed) and complications related to any implanted prosthetic material or the result of the surgical procedure itself is highly recommended. Chartier-Kastler further states that, "The most difficult symptom to assess is postoperative pelvic pain 'induced' by surgery." The development of pelvic pain could be accentuated by a previously undiagnosed preexisting lesion on the spine or other colocalized area, such as the hip. If corrective surgery is being considered, a multidisciplinary approach for diagnostic assessment is highly recommended. [Read more in section B. What Tests and Procedures Are Commonly Performed to Test for Urological Problems?]

Causes and Distribution within the Neurogenic Overactive Bladder cohort of 46,271 patients

- Spinal Cord Injury (SCI) – 4.3% (1,972)
- MS – 17.2% (7,971)
- Parkinson's disease (PD) – 14.9% (6,874)
- Cerebral Palsy (CP) – 2% (929)
- Spina bifida (SB) – 3% (1,400)
- Caude Equina Syndrome – 8.9% (4,110)
- Paralytic Syndrome (quadriplegia) – 7.8% (3,624)
- Hemiplegia/Hemiparesis, stroke complications – 6.2% (2,871)
- Malignant or benign neoplasm of the spinal cord – 1% (481)
- Paralysis of the bladder – 0.3% (154)
- MS plus SCI – 0.1% (37)[1]

II. Dear Biosleuth,

What tests and procedures are commonly performed to test for urological problems?

There are many tests and procedures commonly used to test for urological integrity and problems. Among the most common are urinalysis and urodynamic testing.

Urinalysis

Urinalysis was the first laboratory test performed in the history of medicine and has been used for several thousand years. The urologist orders urinalysis to better understand the integrity of the urological system and possible problems occurring in the kidneys and bladder. To guarantee accuracy, the urine sample must be analyzed while it is fresh, as it can quickly change composition, especially if there are bacteria in the sample. The laboratory examines the color of urine and its chemical composition and looks for the presence of blood cells, urinary crystals, and bacteria, using a microscope.

In JoAnne's case, a urinalysis was all it took to understand that she was dealing with a bladder problem in the first place. The results of urinalysis after a routine physical at her doctor's office provided the ultimate clue to the cause of the stomach pain she suffered for ten years before her diagnosis. Because red blood cells and leukocytes were found in her sample, the doctor knew that the urinary tract was compromised.

Bacterial Culture

Your doctor may order the laboratory to prepare a culture of the fresh urine sample you provide, especially if an infection is suspected. This means the laboratory technician will remove a tiny sample of the urine using a sterile loop which will be streaked across a nutrient-rich medium. Depending on the growth characteristics of bacteria that are present in the sample, the laboratory can identify the bacteria and determine which antibiotics are best able to kill it.

Urodynamic Testing

JoAnne's urologist administered a number of tests to assess the health of her kidneys, ureters, bladder, and urethra. Prior to her visit to the office, she had never even heard of an urodynamic test, so she made a point of learning all she could about these series of tests. JoAnne blogged, "I wonder, as I am sitting in an examination chair, my perineum eye-level to the person conducting the test, exactly what are you looking for? . . A number of leads were placed 'down south' to test my muscle and nerve activity. The test would also measure the actual capacity of my bladder."

Tip Time:

Just as JoAnne's urologist urges her to bring in a clean sample for urinalysis whenever she feels a bladder infection coming on, so may your doctor. Talk to him or her about it. Keep a supply of sterile urine containers on hand, and plan to stop by the laboratory immediately to leave the sample. Fresh is better, so it may be best to take your catheter with you to the laboratory and provide an on-site sample.

Urodynamic Testing[1] is commonly administered to study the causes of many symptoms, including painful urination, urine leakage, recurrent bladder infections, bed wetting, frequent urination, or any number of others. It is a test that most undergoing urological testing eventually have. "My doctor told me that my urodynamic test was important because, in the end, it could indicate [not only the basis for my condition, but] the cause of my Neurogenic Bladder," JoAnne recalls.

When discussing her test results, JoAnne confided, "I have a thick line at the bottom of my graph which, I am told, means that the urine does not willingly empty [from my bladder]. I spent so many years pushing my urine that the strain really shows in the test [result] by a very thick line on the graph. I found that particular fact most interesting and illuminating, of all the results my doctor shared with me."

Urodynamic tests[1] determine:

- Urination Frequency
- Quality of emptying (fully or incompletely)
- Volume and speed of urine voiding
- The flow of urine
- The amount of liquid your bladder can hold; at what point the urge to pee sets in
- The pressure point of any occurring leakage; the effect of coughing or sneezing on leakage
- Nerve impulses

There are many types of urodynamic tests and procedures that your urologist can choose to administer. They can involve different types of imaging equipment, such as x-ray, videos, and ultrasound. Urodynamic testing actually refers to a panel of tests that a urologist uses to better understand any pathology of the urinary tract[1]. Doctors utilize different urodynamic procedures customized for each patient's needs, based on symptoms and the patient consult. Two common procedures are the Filling Cytometry test and "Pressure-Flow "studies, (discussed below). We will also briefly describe some of the other tests that your urologist may wish to perform.

Knowledge Nugget:

The average interior volume/intravesical pressure[2] of a bladder is 40 ml/cm H_2O (varying from 20 to 60 ml/cm H_2O). Your "baseline" level is compared to the volume of urine held as a function of pressure measured during filling and/or voiding of your bladder.

Pressure-Flow Studies

These tests simultaneously measure bladder pressure and the flow rate during the voiding phase of urination, the "micturition cycle." They are used to assess the process of bladder emptying. For example, obstruction of urine outflow can be diagnosed if there is a low urinary flow rate in conjunction with a raised pressure in the bladder during voiding.

Filling Cytometry

Filling Cytometry is a part of urodynamic testing in which the bladder is slowly filled with liquid while pressure and volume measurements are taken. It is a standard for the assessment of bladder function.

Other Common Tests

Electromyography (EMG) is measurement of the electrical activity in the bladder neck (the base of the bladder that empties into the urethra).

Fluoroscopy (moving video x-rays) of the bladder and bladder neck taken while the bladder empties.

Multichannel Cytometry or Cystometrogram (CMG)[1] – measures the pressure in the rectum and in the bladder simultaneously, using two pressure catheters, to deduce the presence of contractions of the bladder wall during bladder filling or other processes. Stress Incontinence can also be tested using a cough or "Valsalva maneuver," which will determine the actual strength of the urethral sphincter. By understanding how hard the bladder muscle is squeezing and monitoring your bladder over time, the urologist will be able to determine if the bladder puts undue strain on your kidneys.

Post-void residual volume test begins with the insertion of a urinary catheter/transducer following the complete emptying of the bladder by the patient. The urine volume is measured (this shows how efficiently the bladder empties). High volumes (180 ml) may be associated with urinary tract infections[3], and they are often associated with patients who experience overflow incontinence.

Ultrasonography – an imaging tool that often reveals congenital abnormalities, for instance, within the kidneys and ureters, which connect/drain urine from the kidneys into the bladder.

Urethral Pressure Profilometry – measures how tightly the sphincter muscle can squeeze.

Urethra Tube Assessment – determines the "tightness" along the length of the urethra (where the urine drains out from the bladder.)

III. Dear Biosleuth,

Do cranberry products help prevent bladder infections?

Our immune systems prevent infections that potentially occur from our daily encounter with invisible assailants (in the microscopic world). We literally live surrounded by bacteria and viruses; our immune systems successfully stave off infections that assault us every day of our lives. (How cool is that?) When the immune system or our bodies' outer defenses (or from within) break down, they are compromised or working overtime – that's when we have big problems.

There are ways we can help boost our immune system, especially when we have become more vulnerable to infection. Maintaining good nutrition is a basic way to provide your body with all the building blocks necessary to live and help prevent stress to the system. Anyone who has to self-catheterize is potentially providing an entry point for bacteria. The body was not designed for the introduction of foreign objects upward through the ureters into the bladder. The system is designed to provide an outlet for outward flow of urine from a sterile enclosure (the bladder) to the outside, which is covered in "normal flora." As long as the normal flora are kept on the outside, the skin is a barrier to their ability to cause infection.

> *Knowledge Nugget:*
>
> An ultrasound can determine if there is swelling[4] and/or a blockage of stones in the urinary tract

Cranberry juice has for years been thought to boost the immune system's ability to fight off urinary tract infections[1] (UTI) by bacteria. Why? Just as penicillin, produced by a mold, is able to kill some bacteria, cranberries contain compounds (called proanthocyanidins) that interfere with the ability of some bacteria and yeast to attach or adhere to the cells lining the interior of the bladder.[2] Once bacteria have gained entry to a rich nutrient source like the inside of the urinary tract, their first

> *Knowledge Nugget:*
>
> An untreated UTI can even cause problems outside of the urinary tract. During pregnancy, it can lead to a premature birth or high blood pressure, and they usually involve the kidneys.

goal is to attach, in order to start replicating and creating a thriving colony. If they are unable to attach, although they may start multiplying, they will be continually dislodged and then washed out with the constant flow of urine through the bladder and urethra. So, if proanthocyanidins, the compounds in cranberries[3] that are thought to prevent the bacteria's ability to attach and start colonizing the lining of the urinary tract, are present – that is good news for women who suffer from urinary tract infections. The bacteria are defeated before they get started. However, success apparently depends on the type of bacteria that are living just outside the urethra and how susceptible they are to being prevented from sticking. Studies have indicated that women who chronically catheterize are not as likely to respond to the benefits of cranberry juice[2].

A recent review of the clinical literature as a whole concluded that cranberry juice is not effective against the prevention of UTI.[4] A follow-up article in the highly influential JAMA (Journal of the American Medical Association) suggested that this finding may actually be the result of a flaw in the studies that were conducted or the way in which they were analyzed.[5] So, we are left with anecdotal stories of isolated cases in which one woman has success in reducing the number of UTIs with cranberry juice extract, and the next woman has not. Success with cranberry extract is varied and personal. Dr. Oz, who hosts a television talk show on current health topics, is a big fan of the benefits of cranberry juice for the treatment of chronic UTIs.[6] How about you? If you want to check with your doctor and take part in an informal "test" yourself, get some Cranberry Extract – in capsule form, not juice) – and take the dosage twice daily and see if it helps reduce your chronic UTIs. Log your progress by keeping track of each UTI your doctor diagnoses to determine if, over time, you have reduced the number of UTIs you acquire with the nutrients found in cranberries. Share your results with us by submitting your experience on the trudytriumph.com blog under "Ask a Question."

Tip Time:

Simple Ways to Reduce the Likelihood of UTI [17]

- *Don't hold urine in your bladder for long periods of time*
- *Drink lots of water every day (6–8 glasses)*
- *Urinate before and after sexual intercourse; drink water*
- *Clean the outer lips of your vagina and anus daily*
- *Avoid feminine douches and hygiene sprays*
- *Consider alternative options for birth control if you use spermicides*
- *Wear underpants with a cotton crotch; avoid tight-fitting pants that trap moisture and provide bacteria a warm, damp breeding ground*
- *Avoid the bathtub; take running-water showers*

IV. Dear Biosleuth,

What is a fistula?

Fistula refers to the unnatural connection[1] of two "alien organs" (organs that are not normally joined). Deep sores or ulcers within the intestinal tract are likewise considered fistulae and may turn into tracts passages that connect different parts of the intestine abnormally; they affect about 30 percent of people with Crohn's disease.

Fistulae may also tunnel into the surrounding tissues of the bladder, vagina, or skin.

Fistulae can develop from numerous causes, including chronic disease, such as inflammatory bowel disease (IBS), complications from surgery, or from trauma. A tear that connects a woman's uterus and bowel is an example. Fistula in the urogenital tract and rectum is most commonly caused by some sort of trauma. A difficult childbirth can be regarded as a source of trauma. Even the long-term use of catheterization could result in a fistula. The remainder of this short discussion of fistula will pertain to traumatic fistula.

An obstetric fistula develops when the blood supply to the tissues of the vagina and the bladder (and/or rectum) is cut off during prolonged or obstructed labor.[3] The affected cells of those tissues subsequently die, and a hole forms through which urine and/or feces pass, uncontrollably. You can imagine the emotional and psychological trauma that ensues for these women, who are meanwhile dealing with the challenges of a new baby. It is the custom, in some countries, for girls to marry extremely young – too young to give birth. The pelvis is not developed, and labor can be prolonged, lasting days. The damage of torn bowel, bladder, vaginal wall, and even a broken pelvis, is profound and can occur. Vaginal fistula, an undoubtedly devastating condition, affects an estimated two million girls and women across Africa and Asia.[4] It would be difficult to estimate the number affected over the centuries. Before modern surgical procedures became available, the brokenness would never have been repaired and the girls/women would have become outcasts. Even now, there is an absence of access to help for many who need it. Because of this, they can be susceptible to chronic infections from the continuous leakage of feces and urine.

Vesicovaginal and rectovaginal fistulae may also be caused by rape. A seemingly unfathomable high number of women in war-torn areas have suffered fistulae after being gang raped and/or raped by the insertion of foreign objects into their genital openings. You may have heard about the cases that turned up after the five-year conflict in Congo ended. In 2003, thousands of women turned out for treatment of traumatic fistulae, caused by systematic, violent gang rape.[5] So many cases were reported that the destruction of the vagina is considered a war injury in Africa, and doctors record it as "a crime of combat."

In the US, both scenarios are hard to comprehend, but in the developing world, the problem is so pronounced that there are Fistula Hospitals. A case study published in 2002[6] looked at fifty-five women in a Fistula Hospital in Ethiopia. These women had all developed obstetric genitourinary fistula, following delivery of their babies. The study found that there was a high rate of success in closure of fistulae, but the development of urinary incontinence or an altered fecal continence was a common consequence of surgery.[7] Extensive reconstruction of the vagina is one of the proposed risk factors for the development of incontinence.[6] Post-operative urethral catheterization using the Foley catheter is a standard among surgeons in the Fistula Hospitals, but the diameter and composition of the catheter varies, and the duration before removal varied, depending on the size of the fistula, from five to forty-two days.[5] Urodynamic testing was utilized to determine that the majority manifested stress incontinence, followed by mixed incontinence and unstable contraction of the bladder muscle.

V. Dear Biosleuth,

Are stem cell therapies available for bladder disease?

There is much hope that the directed use of stem cells will enable doctors to renew damaged organs or repair neurological function in patients with trauma or age-related disease. How? Why? The hope lies in the ability of stem-cell therapy to harness the amazing regenerative power of the human body. If body parts that are no longer functioning or are partially impaired could be restored, this therapy could be a new sort of miracle cure. It would replace organ-transplantation surgery. As of spring 2015, there are ongoing research studies examining the usefulness of stem-cell therapy for bladder diseases. So, therefore, at this time, I would have to answer the question, "Maybe." There are studies underway to determine if alterations of the bladder due to disease/trauma can be alleviated or possibly reversed using stem-cell therapy.

Stem-cell research is a topic of great interest around the globe. Diseases that may potentially benefit are diverse, and the potential impact on health is tremendous. In mid-2014, researchers at Columbia University Medical Center reported significant findings using personalized gene therapy with stem-cell technology to treat retinitis pigmentosa,[1] which can lead to blindness. As studies proceed into human trials, the true impact will be understood. There will be hundreds of research findings in the coming decade, for a myriad of ailments, reporting both positive and negative results. So, rather than provide current research findings for bladder disease, which are still in the early stages, the purpose of this section is to provide some background information on stem-cell research. A grasp of some of the common terminology[2] will give you a framework to better understand research descriptions of new reports in this specialized research area.

California (CA) voters approved a proposition in 2004 to create a vehicle to manage the immense funding that was estimated to go into stem-cell research in that state. The California Institute for Regenerative Medicine (CIRM) provides a great deal of information to the public describing research[3] with stem cells and current progress, as well as systems to distribute funding for research to competing research laboratories. As of 2014, the majority of research grants awarded by the CIRM have gone to research on neurological disorders, but a small percentage have also been awarded to studying diseases of the kidney and urinary tract. Stem-cell research to treat ailments of the bladder has primarily been conducted in preclinical rat models, to date. Doing research in animals first helps researchers determine the most promising treatment protocols to pursue in humans. In general, in these studies, the bladder is compromised in a specific manner in an otherwise healthy animal, and, later, the animal is given stem-cell therapy. Then, a careful analysis is done to compare treated animals to animals that did not receive stem-cell therapy.

Many people are unaware that stem-cell therapy does not necessarily have to involve the use of embryos. True – embryonic stem cells were, early on, thought to be the only human cells which lacked designated "programming" that could be induced into cells that have specialized physical properties and functions, those that form functioning organs such as the lung, heart, brain, and bladder. Research has improved our knowledge and understanding of cell biology, and now we know that immature cells exist in organs that constantly replace and replenish their worn-out cells. Red blood cells live approximately four months and must be constantly regenerated. Red blood cells develop from immature stem cells in the marrow of large bones. Bone marrow is populated with immature (stem) cells that are induced to form the different cells that comprise your blood. Some of these immature cells taken from adults (adult stem cells) have the potential to develop into different specialized cells of the body area into which they are placed. They are said to be "multipotent" – capable of converting into different cell types. If the adult stem cells have been genetically modified to behave as very versatile embryonic cells, they are called induced "pluripotent" stem cells (iPS). This new direction for stem-cell therapy in adult cells removes the ethical concerns that have been raised with the use of embryonic stem cells.

A major shortcoming of transplantation is rejection of "foreign" material, which the recipient's own immune system attacks, similar to when you have a viral infection. However, the true beauty of adult stem-cell therapy is that stem cells can be harvested from a patient's own body, from muscle or fat tissue, which is available in abundance. In autologous stem-cell therapy, the stem cells are isolated from the patient and reinjected into the organ that needs repair of that same patient. In addition, the danger of picking up infectious organisms from contaminated donor tissue is eliminated with autologous therapy. Prior to the discovery of HIV and Hepatitis-C viruses, many people became inadvertently infected with these dangerous viruses when they received infected blood or tissues from anonymous donors.[4]

How do researchers envision the use of stem cells to alleviate various diseases and malfunctions within the urinary tract, though? An excellent paper published by Kim, J. H., 2013, reviews the status of research findings for stem-cell therapy in bladder dysfunctions.[5] This review tells of:

- the use of stem cells to treat bladder outlet obstruction (BOO) – alleviating control of urethral sphincter muscles[6]
- muscle contraction in models that simulate an aging bladder[7] or overactive bladder[8]
- gene therapy[9] using stem cells as carrier vehicles
- neural stem-cell reconstitution in spinal-cord injuries[10]
- tissue-engineering organic material that is more stable than mesh implants for treating pelvic organ prolapse
- adding stem cells to a layer of small-intestine cells to partially regenerate a bladder[11]

One small European study of twenty women diagnosed with Stress Urinary Incontinence (SUI) harvested muscle-derived stem cells and injected the purified cell types back into the sphincter muscle and urethral submucosa of each patient.[12] At a two-year follow-up, 80 percent of the women reported they no longer suffered from SUI. This is very encouraging for future studies.

So, what challenges lie ahead for stem-cell therapy? There are certainly many concerns related to the use of stem cells for treatment of disease. One primary concern is ensuring that cells remain localized to the site of injury/disease and that they mature in a controlled manner. Should the stem cells result in uncontrolled growth, cancer could be the result. For bladder-disease therapy, specifically, the exact growth conditions under which stem cells will reliably mature into bladder cells is still unknown. This is certainly an area of research to keep watch upon. As challenges are managed, stem-cell therapy could become a viable treatment option for patients with bladder disease.

VI. Dear Biosleuth,

How do I find valid, relevant medical information?

Searching for Medical Information:

Doctors have an obligation to keep up with a massive amount of information as research and knowledge progress within health care. To give you an idea of the amount of medical information that is available on the topic of Urology alone, 97,554 articles were published in the fifty-four years from 1955 to 2009. Of these, 1,239 articles were cited more than one hundred times by later publications. Citing an article is significant because it shows that it is highly regarded and later referred to and built upon, as knowledge in the field develops. Therefore, when you consider the authority of a publication, the "Citation Index" level is one critical factor to understanding its level of regard by others in the field.

You can help your health-care team by regularly reviewing medical information available for your particular health concerns.

Consider the following when looking for valid information:

- **Source** – is it authoritative? Is it a collaborative effort produced by a group of experts or the personal opinion of one person?
- **Date** – how old is the information? Can you find an alternative-source information that has been updated more recently?
- **Bias of the Information** – is it provided by someone who stands to gain from the information provided? Check for statements of authorship, funding, or source for the information of a site, such as a profit-based organization.

Sources of good information include:

- Nonprofit associations/organizations that pertain to the topic
- US National Institutes of Health (government) resources
- Official Information Resources (e.g., a drug monograph that is approved by the FDA)

READ MORE:

General Consumer Health Information on Medical Topics:
http://www.nlm.nih.gov/medlineplus/medlineplus.html

The National Library of Medicine & NIH provide Medical Texts for you to search and read:
http://www.ncbi.nlm.nih.gov/books

One resource that physicians, administrators, and health plans utilize when determining the standard of care is the "Systematic Review," which provides the latest information and health-care trends/treatments for a particular health condition. By familiarizing yourself with the current systematic-review trends, you can share your understanding with your health-care team and actually speak their language.

The US NIH now provides these on a variety of health topics, and each article includes an easy-to-understand abstract of the latest available information.

TOOL:

DOI Resolver – a numerical shortcut code that navigates your Internet browser directly to a website destination. Enter any doi code you wish to follow here:
https://dx.doi.org

2. Letters from Readers

I was not alone in my frustration to find answers. I received many letters from readers of my blog TrudyTriumph.com. I would like to share a few with you, with their permission, of course. Like me, they were both desperate for answers.

One of the most rewarding opportunities I have as the author of the blog is receiving correspondence from people who have concerns and heartaches, as well as victories, and find solutions for living a full life. I am including several of these letters because they express many of the emotions I dealt with as I was coming to grips with my Neurogenic Bladder and Bowel. They represent the heart of this book.

Daily life is not easy with a Neurogenic Bladder and Bowel. We need to be careful, calculated, and sometimes clock-watchers. At times, we need to say "No" to a fun activity because it would just be too difficult to manage. We try not to complain because we are happy for the full life we have. These correspondences represent people who are making the best of the hand dealt to them.

Sometimes Neurogenic Bladder and Bowel are very difficult to diagnose. That is the hard part. Like me, many NB patients have trouble understanding why their incontinence started in the first place. I still do not know; many of us will never find out. I struggled for years, not realizing that my sacral nerve was compromised and, therefore, my bowel and bladder were not responding normally. My doctors were puzzled as well because my symptoms mirrored other medical problems.

As you read these letters, you will see some of the many causes. Fear, frustration, anxiety, and inspiration are daily companions. The writers of these letters are the fighters they need to be, and, because of that strength, they are shining examples of determination.

Laura, Vaginal Delivery

Laura, as you will see, developed her Neurogenic Bladder and Bowel because of a forceps delivery. She has learned to cope. Besides raising her daughter, she works full-time and does agility training with her dogs. She has found solutions and is making it work. She gets out and goes on with her life. I so admire her spunk and energy.

Dear Trudy,

I am 33 years old, and I gave birth to a healthy baby girl on 20th July 2012. My life changed totally after that day, and I mean it in ways which the majority of parents would not understand.

I had a vacuum-assisted vaginal birth with epidural. It was not a difficult birth, and everything went smoothly until a week after I was discharged from hospital. I realized that I did not feel any fullness in my bladder; neither could I move my bowels. When I went to the restroom, urine would flow, but I had a lack of sensation and could not control my bladder. I had to manually clear my bowels, and it was a horrifying process. I called my gynae immediately but was told that it was normal. So I carried on this way for a month more.

I was referred to a urologist for my bladder problems, and she said that I could be suffering from a UTI, but results of the test for it were negative. So I was put on some antibiotics for the next few days. The side effect of the antibiotic was diarrhea, and it was then I realized my control over my bowels was also lacking greatly. I soiled myself without knowing, and I felt a great sense of despair. I checked myself into hospital and did an MRI scan and X-Ray, as doctors suspected that I might have Cauda Equina Syndrome from the epidural injection area. The results were negative, and I was sent home with a diagnosis of Neurogenic Bladder and Bowel.

Since then, I have tried all sorts of alternative medicines and acupuncture. I have also tried the Percutaneous Tibial Nerve Stimulation (PTNS), in which a needle was inserted into my ankle for twelve sessions. It did not work for me, and my doctor suggested a neuromodulator to implant a device into my body. I am hoping not to do anything too invasive, and I am still looking and hoping for a miracle. I find great joy in caring for my daughter, and I am involved in various sports activities with my dogs, as it keeps my mind off my condition. I have to wake up extra early to clear my bowels and bladder and take note of the nearest restrooms wherever I go. I have avoided traveling too far, as I am afraid to have accidents. I thank Trudy for giving me the opportunity to share about myself to the rest of you who may be looking for answers, like I am.

—Laura

Jennifer, Spinal Cyst

I love Jennifer's letters because she did not give up but kept trying to find the cause of the discrepancy in her leg length and the cause of her Neurogenic Bladder. She is the perfect example of tenacity. I like the steps she lays out in her detailed letter explaining how she found help. She points out that some doctors may tell us we have Multiple Sclerosis, but, in fact, there might be other reasons for our medical woes.

Hi Trudy,

I came across your blog site today and, after reading several posts, found myself moved by your honesty and moral character. (I applaud your stance on the use of stem cells.) I also suffer from Neurogenic Bladder and find myself perusing the Internet (probably too often) in search of answers as to why this is happening to me. I am only 33 years old. My symptoms began more than a year ago and include a combination of spastic bladder/frequency, urinary retention, and nocturia. I've been to many doctors over the last year and, as of October, am finally getting medical care that matters (my first urologist diagnosed me with chronic UTI, sent me away with ninety pills of Bactrim, and told me I had to find a way to medicate and cope with the symptoms myself). Now that I have new, wonderful doctors, I recently had three MRIs: brain, spine, and thoracic, the results of which I will find out tomorrow.

On the eve of my MRI results, your blog could not have come at a better time. In reading your posts, I now understand that my condition may not be tracked to a specific disease or disorder right away, as some of your followers and yourself seem to have been struggling without answers for quite some time. While this realization is somewhat disheartening, I feel that, as a result of reading your story and those of some of your followers, I am better prepared for what my neurologist may or may not say tomorrow. I feel prepared to continue to wait and see, should I have to do so, and feel supported knowing there are other people out there in the same position I am in.

While reading your autoimmune disease post, you state that you may have MS. I was wondering if you've received a diagnosis for this or what course of action your doctors are taking to rule in/out this possibility. If it is not MS causing your symptoms, do your doctors have other conditions/diseases they think may be the cause? I ask because I've typically seen Neurogenic Bladder related to MS (when spinal-cord injury is not a factor) but have been told by doctors that they suspect this is not the case for me. If MS is not the cause, I am wondering what else may be (I've been tested for Lyme and B12 deficiency, both negative).

I was also wondering if you've tried pelvic-floor physical therapy. I've received pelvic-floor physical therapy for my condition since October and find that the manual, internal therapy works best to keep my muscles loose and less spastic (I also get massage and electrical stimulation at PT). I currently go to therapy once a week. As I am still going to therapy, need to continue going to therapy, and have no idea when I'll be able to stop going to therapy, I am wondering if you have experience with pelvic-floor therapy – what your experience is/was like and how long it's lasted. I don't know anyone else with this condition, so I hope you don't mind my asking these questions. I'm just curious to know what the "norm" has been for others – maybe, for some glimmers of hope that this will not be the state of my life for the rest of my life!

In closing, I want to express thanks and gratitude to you for writing your blog and creating a community where people suffering from this frustrating condition can go for information and, thankfully, some humor. You bring light and laughter to this often dark and secretive condition.

I will continue to read your old posts and look forward to the new ones. I hope to hear back from you soon.

Thank you,

–Jennifer

Now, Fellow Travelers, I will explain to you the most important part of this section: bladder issues are sometimes very hard to diagnose, even by good doctors. If you suspect something is wrong, follow your gut. Keep searching and *don't give up!*

I felt so sorry for Jennifer after reading her first letter. Eight months later, I received her second letter. I was happy that she did not have to wonder about her mysterious symptoms any longer. Here is what she said:

Hi Ms. Trudy,

I wrote to you earlier this year – around February, I think. You shared my story on your blog under the name "Marilyn." I am writing you again because after two-plus years I am finally close to a diagnosis/cause of my Neurogenic Bladder. In March, I began experiencing numbness and tingling down my right leg, plus a deep groin pain. I also had an obvious leg-length discrepancy that I was not born with. These symptoms were new and in addition to my already diagnosed Neurogenic Bladder.

My story is very long, as I have been to many doctors, most of whom told me they had never seen anything like this. I have also seen many doctors that told me they could not help me and "wished me luck." Through all of this, I've learned many very important lessons about navigating the medical world: (1) always trust your instinct because you know your body best; (2) never let the doctor convince you that you are imagining things, being overly dramatic, or aren't feeling what you know you are feeling; (3) always get a copy of your records, especially test results/reports; (4) be your #1 advocate and do your research; (5) always get multiple opinions; and (6) never give up!

As I mentioned, my story is very long and has many twists and turns so I'll fast-forward to the present and get to the diagnosis. I've been diagnosed with a very rare arachnoid or Tarlov cyst that is sitting on my spinal cord at the S3, the part of the sacrum responsible for the parasympathetic nerves that control the bladder. The cyst is approximately three inches long, spanning from the S2 to the S4. I say it is either arachnoid or Tarlov's because I received two different opinions from two different radiologists as to what type of cyst it is. I am still in the process of seeing specialists to determine the exact type. These types of cysts cause a wide variety of problems, from bladder issues to radicular pain and can cause permanent nerve damage if not surgically excised.

The only reason this cyst was finally discovered was because an Orthopedic Surgeon (OS) I asked about my leg-length discrepancy and groin pain (I thought they were related symptoms) ordered a neurogram (at my request), which is a type of MRI and a nerve-conduction study. To get the nerve-conduction study, I went back to my regular neurologist. The study was performed and indicated radicular nerve pain on the lower right side (down my leg) of my body.

Now that I had nerve pain, my neurologist was more interested in my case than he was when I first came to his office, presenting with only Neurogenic Bladder. Now that I had his attention, I explained all of my symptoms and showed the doctor the difference in my legs. After hearing my story, he ordered an MRI of my sacrum as he thought something might be hiding in my sacrum. Sure enough, something was — the cyst!!

To make matters worse and more interesting, the cyst did not explain the leg-length discrepancy or the deep groin pain. I had been to several professionals about these symptoms. All of them said nothing was wrong with me despite the fact that they measured my legs and could tell they were unequal (there's about a 1.5 inch difference between the right and left leg), they could see my right leg turning inward, and I had an MRI of my pelvis (the neurogram the first OS ordered) that indicated something could be wrong with my hip (the radiologist couldn't say for sure what/if something was wrong because the MRI was designated for the pelvic/nerves and not the hip).

Thank God for my neurologist, because he was the only doctor who would listen to me about the groin pain and leg-length discrepancy, and the only doctor who ordered me an MRI to look specifically at my right hip. In addition to the cyst, the MRI revealed that I have Grade III chondromalacia and a labral tear in the right hip joint. This diagnosis explained the groin pain I was having and the leg-length discrepancy.

So where am I now? Well, I am looking at two surgeries, one to repair my hip (I may need a total hip replacement; I'm still seeing an OS to determine what to do) and the other to remove the cyst. Luckily, the hip issue is common, so it is an easy fix. The cyst, on the other hand, has proven more difficult and has taken me to a whole new realm of the medical world – what I like to call the Super Specialty Specialist realm.

This is the realm of doctors who are so specialized that they:

1. usually don't take insurance
2. will only see you if they are "interested" in your case

I say "interested" because that is what my neurologist always says. He says that with rare diseases, you have to find a doctor that is "interested" in both your disease and in helping you specifically So that is where I am at right now: trying to find a doctor who is interested and who is willing to help me. My neuro did refer me to a Super Specialized neurologist at a very prestigious hospital, who is supposed to help with coordinating my care for both the hip and the cyst. I need a coordinator because the doctors have to be sure which symptoms are caused by my hip and which are caused by the cyst. I believe this is to justify the spine surgery because the spine surgery is risky due to nerve roots that may be tethered or entangled with the cyst.

I called the doctor's office and, like the rookie I am in navigating the Super Specialty Specialist realm, tried to make an appointment to see him. I was told that he would not consider seeing me until I sent him all of my medical records and test results. I've sent my records to his office and am now crossing my fingers that he will be "interested" in my case and willing to help me. He is just the first step though. I still have to find a neurosurgeon who will be "interested" and willing to help me. So that's the short version of my story. I wanted to send you an update because I hope that my story can help someone else. I also wanted to share because many doctors tried to make me feel like everything was in my head. I was also turned away by many doctors.

Having an issue like Neurogenic Bowel or Bladder is frustrating enough without having doctors that either won't help you because they aren't interested in your case or dismiss you as delusional or whiny because they can't solve your problem in fifteen minutes. Hopefully my story can help motivate those who may be struggling to keep pushing for a diagnosis or help someone who may have Neurogenic Bladder/Bowel know that there are other diagnoses out there besides MS (I heard on more than one occasion that I either had MS or that nothing was really wrong with me).

I appreciate you taking the time to listen to my story and helping those of us suffering with this often-irritating disability. The community you foster through your blog is very helpful, especially when it feels like nobody else on this earth understands what I'm going through.

Keep on keepin' on :) Many Thanks!!!
—Jennifer

Knowledge Nugget:

Health care systems vary from state to state and country to country. Regardless of where you live, it is worthwhile to take time to understand how your health plan works, so you can make the best use of the system you have.

I have another e-mail I would like to share with you from another dear person dealing with the anguish of not knowing but suffering real symptoms. My favorite part of his letter is his "really-wanting-to-help-himself" attitude. Lewis is from Great Britain, so he works with a different health-care system than those of us who live in the US. He says he has to wait longer and has fewer choices. He is proactive and doing his best. He ends his letter, "I hope the letter finds you happy and in good health." I love that because, like Lewis, I do see myself as a happy person and in good health.

Lewis, Unknown

Hi Trudy,

I found your blog yesterday after finding your profile on "patients like me," which I've recently joined, and I've just read the whole thing from end to end. As I have Neurogenic Bladder and Bowel myself, it all resonated very strongly for me, so I thought I would drop you a line.

I was diagnosed with Neurogenic Bladder last September, after becoming, suddenly, very incontinent about a year ago. In the space of a week, for no known reason, I went from totally normal to complete loss of bladder control at the beginning of April 2012, and it was absolutely devastating and humiliating.

I live in the UK, so my health-care setup is a little different from yours, and, while I don't have to pay anything, it is *much* slower, so it was four months before I was able to see a specialist who told me that, as well as the incontinence, I also had significant retention. Urodynamic testing showed that my bladder wasn't contracting at all, but, as it fills and the pressure increases, the sphincter will spontaneously loosen and release just enough to lower the pressure, and this was happening about once an hour, up to a cupful at a time. The rest was just sitting there in my bladder, going stale, and I had two UTIs in six months as a result, so I was put onto catheters at the end of September.

Like you, my "training" was short and limited, although I was given a DVD and a free mirror. At this point I need to let you into my little "secret" – I'm a pre-op transsexual man, which means that while I look, think, and feel like a man, I was born female, and I haven't yet had any genital surgery, so I still have female "plumbing." I had to laugh at your blog entry about needing three hands to do it with the mirror, and I very quickly learned with practice to do it without needing to look.

I started with four times a day, but that wasn't enough to keep the pressure in my bladder low enough to prevent further incontinence, so, last month, my doctor recommended I go up to six times a day, and that is much better for me. Unlike you, I have no internal sensation in my bladder at all, and I don't even feel pressure or pain when it's full, so I go strictly by the clock – once every three hours. I still get occasional leaks though, especially after a couple of pints in the pub (I've learned to take extra catheters with me when I do that. One extra catheter per pint of beer seems to work!).

Bowel issues started also around August; I noticed that I was pooping much less often than normal, and, when I did need to go, I wouldn't be aware of it until too late, sometimes with the predictable consequences if I wasn't close enough to a toilet. I usually get around fifteen to twenty minutes warning, which is enough most of the time but not always. I generally "go" about once every five to six days, and, on days that I do go, I tend to go twice. Oddly, I'm never constipated, and I don't need a stool softener.

As well as the bladder and bowel problems, I have other symptoms, too. That made me think "MS." For several years, I've had issues on-and-off with extreme muscle fatigue in my leg, and pins-and-needles in my hands and feet, sometimes to the extent that I need a cane when I go out. I never mentioned this to my doctor before (I'd be laughed at and thrown out if I went to my GP with pins-and-needles), but I mentioned it to my urologist, who said that my problems are clearly neurological in origin, so I was sent for an MRI scan in October. That came back all-clear, so I have no spinal or brain tumors, no damaged discs, and no sign they could see of MS, which was something of a relief. I understand that sometimes MS doesn't show on an MRI scan even when present, so I suppose it still might be that. Now it appears that I've been "written off" by the urologist – I've had all the tests that are available to me on the NHS, and they've basically said, "We don't know the cause, and we're not going to pursue it any further unless there is a serious deterioration in your symptoms," so now I'm under the care of my local Continence Service, which helps me manage my condition by diet and routine. They normally also recommend kegel exercises, but, in my case, I can't do that at all; my pelvic-floor muscles are completely paralyzed.

Your blog has also inspired me to try managing my condition by alternative therapy, and I am definitely going to start a regimen of B-12 and cranberry supplements. I can't get D-mannose here locally, and I can get fresh cranberries only in December (they're imported for Christmas and they're horrendously expensive), but I can get cranberry juice, dried fruit, and pills. I had a third UTI in January, and I'm anxious to avoid any more; because I can't feel anything in there, I can't tell when I have one except that my pee goes very cloudy. I had the beginnings of another, I think, about two weeks ago, but a week of intensive cranberry-juice drinking seems to have cleared it up without having to resort to antibiotics. I'm also going to try a zinc supplement, as zinc is known to have an impact on nerve health.

Another part of your blog that I loved was your piece about the "go-girl" device. As a trans-man, being able to pee standing up is a "big thing," and I've tried similar devices before. Over here, we have one called the "She-Whizz," which is sold in camping/outdoor sports stores. Why do these things always have such terrible puns for names? Unfortunately, I never found one that didn't leak out the back if you're not very careful to pee very, very slowly, so I quickly gave up that idea. Now that I'm using catheters, I find standing to pee much easier; in fact, trying to do it sitting down is near-impossible, so I always stand now. I will even use a public urinal sometimes, if no one else is in there when I start. I use the VaPro Advance catheter, which has a protective sleeve so that no part of the actual catheter is exposed before insertion. The intention is to reduce any chance of infection. It's also about four inches longer than a standard female catheter; this means that I can guide it in with my fingers more easily, and I've mastered the art of inserting it through the fly of my pants/underpants, even when wearing a pad or nappy (provided that it's dry), without having to pull it all down to my knees. So there's at least one bonus to having a Neurogenic Bladder, for me.

Anyway, I just wanted to say again that I love your blog, I find it very entertaining and informative, and I really hope you keep writing regularly.

Hope this finds you happy and in good health.

Kind regards,

—Lewis

Beth, Stroke

What I just love about Beth's letter is her willingness to share her frustration about the stigma we live with as we deal with bladder and bowel disorders. She imagines herself telling the world on You Tube exactly what it is like. I admire that. It is just what I did when I started my blog. Now, you know my name because it is connected with this book, but, for years, most of you knew me as Trudy. I admit I was ashamed of my bladder and bowel condition. I did not want to be the butt of jokes; I did not want people to snicker when they saw me. Yet here is Beth. She, like me, is tired of the stigma and wants to do something about it. I applaud her.

Dear Trudy,

People living with bladder and bowel difficulties are ridiculously stigmatized. I've rarely spoken about it. I could count the people I've told (other than doctors) on one hand. I don't plan on spreading the word about my Neurogenic Bladder to everyone I know, but I am seriously thinking about making some videos explaining my struggle.

I had a stroke eleven years ago that wreaked major havoc on some functions of my nether regions. The incontinence has improved a bit on its own, and I've learned strategies to keep myself a little drier. But at the same time, the leakiness level varies. There are days to weeks (!) that my faithful ultrathin stays pretty dry, with just a little dampness at the end of the day. Other times, I'm changing that pad three times a day (sometimes my underwear and bottoms with it). Sometimes I can "hold it," and, other times, the urge/spasm is so strong, my muscles do no good. I've never had to cath, but I did have problems emptying occasionally. I've tried medications, timed voids, biofeedback; nothing really worked. I'm young. I'm thirty-four now, and this started when I was twenty-three.

For the last decade, I have worn pads and elastic-waist pants most of the time. Without both of them, I'm afraid I might not be able to make it to the bathroom in time when my bladder wants a little exercise (spasm). Often, I didn't make it in time. I've wet myself countless times, soaked right through the pad. Many times, I'll walk up to my door, and, as I put the key in, I feel my bladder hollering, "Hey! Hey you! Time to go!" The urgency is so bad I'm holding myself – doing the pee-pee dance. Despite this, I don't make it across the living room without urine running over the pad's capacity, down my leg, and often leaving little puddles.

ONE OF THE MANY REASONS I LIKE TILE FLOORS IN MY HOME.

When I finally make it to the bathroom, after attempting to walk with my bad balance and crazy leg (I have gait problems also, and walking and bladder spasms don't mix well in my book), sometimes I piss like a racehorse. And sometimes my bladder is like, "Oh, what was the rush? I already went. You should change your pants and clean up with a wet towel." Thanks a lot.

Right now I'm on the fence about putting a pacemaker in my butt or getting something that includes the word "toxin" injected onto the aforementioned nether regions. Not too excited about either of those, but I've exhausted other options. I have an interstim stage 1 scheduled in a week, and the more I read and think about it, the more I want to cancel. There are just too many things that can go wrong there that don't have much to do with the actual surgery. If that makes any sense.

I appreciate the humor and candor of your blog; it's definitely the first one on the topic that I've really enjoyed. I don't see why this page doesn't have more likes. Wish me luck, and I hope to talk to ya soon.

–Beth

Janine, Cushing Syndrome

I find Janine's letter so sad because she suffered a spinal-cord infarction due to her many surgeries. Her letter explains that the cause of Neurogenic Bladder and Bowel can be rooted in an apparently unrelated event. Her letter reminds me that Neurogenic Bladder can happen any time to anyone, so why in the world don't we talk about it more? Janine is lovely and upbeat and helps me understand another's walk.

Dear Trudy,

Before describing the effects of Cushing Syndrome or Disease on my bladder and bowels, I feel it only fair to give a "Readers Digest" condensed-version definition of the condition. Cushing syndrome is a disease caused by an abnormally high presence of cortisol in the body. Cortisol is a steroid produced by the adrenal glands. Unfortunately, excess cortisol (hypercortisolism) leads to a myriad of unpleasant symptoms, the most common being drastic weight gain, especially in the midsection, while maintaining thin arms and legs. Other symptoms may include but are not limited to excessive body hair (hirsutism), buffalo hump, moon-shaped face, purple stretch marks (striae), fragile skin that bruises easily, acne, slow healing, missing periods (amenorrhea), high blood pressure, depression, diabetes, osteoporosis, fatigue, and muscle weakness. Cushing's patients are often misdiagnosed and can wait years for the correct diagnosis, due to the overlap of symptoms with other diseases.

Diabetes is the result of overproduction of cortisol, which can induce high blood sugar. Anyone who has lived with diabetes knows that excessive thirst and urination come along with it. Most Cushing patients will tell you they wake up multiple times during the night to void and tend to have a tremendous output of urine. Also, people with Cushing may do something called "cycling." This means that their cortisol will be tremendously high at some points and tremendously low at others. Low cortisol can cause diarrhea, nausea, and incredible stomach upset.

My own experience has been slightly different from the norm. I had tumors on one adrenal gland that were causing the excess cortisol; however, I also had tumors on the other adrenal gland, causing excess aldosterone. Aldosterone is another steroid produced by the adrenal glands that directly affects the breakdown and absorption of salt in the body. You would be surprised by just how important this is. Not only does hyperaldosterone cause extremely high blood pressure, but it creates something called "salt-wasting." The excessive urination is so intense that potassium and salt just come right out in the urine and lead to a state of low potassium (hypokalemia), which can be extremely dangerous if not treated.

I mentioned that people with Cushing tend to wait a long time for a diagnosis. I became sick at the age of nineteen. I doubled in weight in less than a year, and my blood pressure was easily running 200/95 most days. Yet my doctor continued to feed me blood-pressure medication until the age of twenty-three. He finally figured that maybe I wasn't just being lazy, overeating, or very depressed. He sent me to a nephrologist, who scanned my kidneys to see if my arteries were narrowed and causing my high blood pressure. Thank goodness, he finally did! The nephrologist saw something called an abdominal aortic aneurysm (AAA) in the scan and had me immediately admitted to the hospital. An AAA is no joke. It is basically when the aorta is under such immense pressure for such a long time that it sort of splits and balloons out. The situation allowed the blood to channel through two openings. The ballooning of the outer wall of the second opening led to its weakened condition. In the elderly, it is much weaker and subject to bursting. I should have been dead. My young age is what saved me.

The hospital that discovered my AAA was not equipped to deal with such a matter, so they transferred me to a city hospital. The first course of treatment was to assess the damage and lower my blood pressure. An endocrinologist walked in, took one look at me. and was able to surmise I had Cushing. He was right. I was a textbook example of someone with Cushing. Within the year, I had my right adrenal gland fully removed and my left one mostly removed. They left behind a piece of the left, hoping it may someday be able to function again on its own. The withdrawal I went through from steroids after surgery was intense. When a person has his adrenal glands removed, he may be dependent on steroids for life. Without those steroids, he can go into a state of adrenal insufficiency, or "AI." AI is a serious matter. Among the more serious symptoms are diarrhea, nausea, and vomiting. I was lucky, because, when my surgeons saved my partial adrenal, it eventually continued to make aldosterone. That meant I only needed to replace cortisol, putting me at lower risk for AI.

The presence of the AAA prior to the adrenalectomies had, unfortunately, resulted in the need for additional surgery; it needed to be repaired. I went in for surgical grafting of my aorta in November 2006. Everything that could go wrong did. I had infections, was in and out of surgery, but, most importantly for our purpose here, suffered a spinal-cord infarction. Something like that had always been a risk of the surgery, but I never thought it would happen to me. I remember feeling very tired and unable to get out of my hospital bed. Then, I woke up . . . and was unable to feel my legs. I was paralyzed from the waist down. They told me that the fluid in my spine had been temporarily blocked – that I may never walk again. Not only did I have this gaping hole in my side in which they were still continuing to operate every other day to debride the wound, in an attempt to rid me of infection, but now I was paralyzed!

I was extremely lucky, in the sense that I gradually regained feeling in my legs. When I say "gradually," I don't mean it was a slow sense of awareness of my legs: it was extremely slow and painful. I also began physical therapy. During that time, I had a catheter in, and my bowels had become impacted. The impaction was horrible. I had a very nasty and not well-meaning nurse manually remove the impaction. It was both humiliating and painful. I will never forget her long fingernails. Turns out, this would become commonplace. My bowels were flaccid. So they started giving me so many stool softeners that I learned quickly that I had no control over my bowels. I was constantly having accidents and started wearing diapers. Next, they removed my catheter. I had to pee so badly, and I just couldn't. I didn't understand. I had no idea this could happen. I remember sitting on the toilet in my room running my hand under warm water from the sink, just praying I would pee. Nothing happened. The nurses would come in and straight-cath me. Unfortunately, I have always had a large urine output, with or without Cushing, so the four to six hours they considered a normal interval between cathing would set me into a state of agony. My bladder was so full, and I was in so much pain, pleading with them to cath me. Their responses, "You can't need to be cathed again." Finally, a kidney doctor came in and said there was nothing wrong. I just had a larger volume than most and that they should restrict my fluid intake. I had my water held ransom and, because of the paralysis, couldn't get up to get any. The result was that I was still putting out an abnormal amount of urine, and I became dehydrated. They returned my water to me.

The hardest part in all this was learning how to catheterize myself. The therapist tried to help me. She gave me a mirror and told me to lie in bed and do it with a self-contained kit. Ummm, I weigh more than 300 pounds. I haven't seen my urethra since I was nineteen. Are you kidding me? I would just stab at myself, upset and blind, because I had to pee so bad. Not to mention, I couldn't help but think, "How would I ever do anything in the real world if I constantly had to do this?" Then I would have to beg the nurses to do it for me. Forget sleep. This would happen every couple of hours, because I had to go so often. I was so lucky because I met this wonderful woman with MS in therapy who said she had been cathing for years. She was a little bit on the heavier side, but not as big as me, and said she used these little "14 French sticks" and emptied her bladder right into the toilet. She described to me how she did it, and it was only a short while before I was able to do it, too! I am forever thankful to her for teaching me what the therapists and doctors could not!

So, skipping ahead to a couple of years later: I had discovered a bowel plan that was not perfect but acceptable. However, my cathing frequency was becoming my biggest issue. I had been cathing upward of thirty times a day! I could not take a half-hour car ride without being so uncomfortable I wanted to cry. Not to mention the infections . . . I always had one. I decided to see a local urologist. I told her all of my symptoms and what I had been through, and she did not even have to physically examine me. She gave me a bunch of pamphlets and a video and explained interstim implants and sacral stimulation. She said it would get my frequency under control and that there was a good chance I would pee again. Six surgeries later . . . Yes, I said SIX, and $3,000 later, the implants had not helped at all, and they were burning under the skin. I won't get into the details of why I had so many surgeries, but let's just say she sold me on the false hope she gave, because I was so desperate. She had even gone as far as to let me believe the implants would improve my bowel function. I felt betrayed. I had also gained back the 100 pounds I had lost prior to their insertion, due to all the depression and recuperation from the surgeries. I had to start going to pain-management classes because the weight was causing too much stress on my surgical sites in both my ribs and abdomen.

Fast-forwarding again, to about two more years later (about two-and-a half-years ago): I decided to see a urologist in the city. He was very nice and said we needed to do something called a urodynamic study so that he could assess the extent of my bladder function. He was extremely honest and blunt in his assessment. He said that the interstim implants could **never** have helped me. I was both devastated and relieved by his honesty. He basically explained that the nerve damage caused by my spinal infarction was causing my nerves to work overtime, trying to stimulate my bladder. He further explained that the damage was too severe for me to ever push out urine on my own again. The best course of action was for me to try to control the frequency of my urination with medication. I tried so many medications and still only got down to cathing around twenty times a day. He also said that he would remove the implants for me whenever I wanted.

Not much time had passed, and I was constantly online, looking for any sort of new procedure that might help me at all. It had escalated to the point that I began leaking if I didn't make it to a bathroom in time. Finally, I came across an article on botox. I called my urologist immediately and asked him if I was a candidate. He said I was, and he scheduled me. I had the botox-injection treatments and interstim implants removed at the same time.

Here I am, two-and-a-half years later. I just had my fifth set of botox injections, and I am so much more content. I am only cathing an average of ten to fifteen times a day. I don't leak anymore, either. It's still not perfect or ideal, but so much better than before. My bladder isn't running my life. I get the series of shots about every six months, in the hospital under "twilight." Some patients have it done right in his office without any sedation, but I am not interested in finding out what twenty or thirty some-odd shots to my bladder feel like without sedation. I will say that I am always on the lookout for the next best advancement.

I wanted to share my story with all of you. No one should have to endure all of this unnecessary pain, embarrassment, humiliation, and just plain life-threatening danger. Had I known anything about Cushing prior to my diagnosis, there is a very good chance so much of this could have been avoided. Think of this as a cautionary tale. I cannot emphasize how important it is to educate yourself. If I have taken anything away from my experience, that would be it. It's OK to question things. Doctors are people, just like us. Some are good, and some are not so good.

All the best,

—Janine

I want to thank all of these thoughtful people for their caring letters. They are fine examples of marvelous individuals who want to help others by sharing their experiences. Please, let's end the self-imposed isolation and do our part in spreading the word that this is a common condition and that it is OK to talk about it. By sharing with each other, we can help others who are struggling with this challenging and often overwhelming condition.

3. Thoughts To Leave With You

13 For thou hast possessed my reins: thou hast covered me
in my mother's womb.
14 I will praise thee; for I am fearfully and wonderfully made: marvelous
are thy works; and that my soul knoweth right well.

—Psalm 139:13-14 [Authorized (King James) Version]

—by "Biosleuth" Julia Parker

What a wonder the human body is! The functions of more than 100 trillion cells are not only maintained but also coordinated through the various organs and systems they comprise, by signals sent out over nerve pathways originating in the brain[1]. Our bodies endure a lifetime of stresses that affect some systems more than others, depending on circumstances and our ability to adapt to the environmental factors we encounter. Although human bodies all share a basic blueprint, no two people are exactly the same. Each of us is affected by our genetics, gender, age, and environment. The sum of these factors creates our health picture. Despite all that we throw at them – both physically and emotionally – our bodies continue to function, but eventually injury or stress can surpass the body's many defenses and repair systems, and we develop illness or aches and pains we never experienced in our youth.

Neurogenic Bladder, the altered control of urination from the bladder due to interruption of the nerve signals to components of the bladder and thus urination, itself, is a special case of Incontinence, "difficulty controlling the flow of urine"[2]. In other words, it is incontinence with a neurologic component. There is much more information made public under the label "Incontinence" than "Neurogenic Bladder," but the social stigmas are the same, as are many of the symptoms and coping mechanisms of the two. Although Neurogenic Bladder can be managed, it is a serious concern, and its symptoms are often not promptly dealt with (or even discussed with a health-care provider), so it is likely not diagnosed until damage has been done.

In simpler, more familiar terms, let's compare the bladder to an automatic-flush toilet that you've used in the airport, your favorite movie theatre, or sports arena. These systems are designed to speed up the process by "sensor-control." When they stop functioning, it can be due to a mechanical issue (the pipes or toilet are stopped up), or the electrical system is no longer working. If the system is not working, and fluids continue to build within the toilet, it will overflow or back up. Similar things are happening with the Neurogenic Bladder. There are no signals, there is a disconnect, two perfect parts that lack the communication system to allow them to work together.

This book provides the real account of JoAnne's journey from initial symptoms and diagnosis, through the exploration of her risk factors, and ultimately to the adjustments she has made to live her new normal life with a serious, chronic health condition. Her struggle to find reasons for her chronic pelvic pain ultimately led her to the discovery that she had a Neurogenic Bladder and Bowel. Her desire to share not only her many frustrations but also how she has been able to reclaim her life and return to an active lifestyle ultimately led to the writing of this book. Through the process of sharing her experiences, challenges, and victories with others, she discovered new purpose; this book has been part of her journey to healing, both emotionally and spiritually. We hope that this book will provide insight, encouragement and/or inspiration that will aid you in your own walk through life's changes.

When JoAnne decided to write this book, she asked me if I thought the project was viable and if I was interested in helping her. After giving it some thought, I told her that based on the lack of information available for the patient with a Neurogenic Bladder, I thought it was a great idea, except that neither of us had ever taken on a project of this magnitude. Besides compiling the basic information we wanted to include, we decided the best format was one in which JoAnne shared her story in the form of a narrative, with occasional interjections of information or "Knowledge Nuggets." Those would be my primary contribution. By combining these two styles, we hoped to appeal to a wider audience, depending on the reader's need for encouragement or valid information they may lack.

Despite the fact that so many people are affected with conditions that impact the urinary system, it is difficult to find reliable information, especially if one is not familiar with powerful, specialized search tools that guard access to current medical information. Frustration finally led to JoAnne's decision to share her medical condition with me: someone outside of her family and medical team: a trusted friend and experienced medical librarian. She was comfortable talking to me about her situation since I was both a good listener and willing to help her learn more through medical-literature searches. I have been able to serve as both confidante and consultant. The launch of her Internet blog, under the penname "Trudy" has served to attain the primary goal of reaching others living with bladder and bowel problems, and to share their story and, perhaps, compare notes.

JoAnne continues her blog for which she seeks out topics that resonate with others dealing with matters of continence on a practical basis. Past topics have included how to be prepared to deal with a Neurogenic Bladder in public places, how she discovered the perfect catheter to fit her lifestyle, and how important it is to guard against infections. She continues to find herself with no lack of subject matter. Over time, more people have discovered the blog and responded to her posts.

The blog has also provided a forum for readers to submit questions. We have included a few of them, along with detailed answers in Part II of this book, under the heading of "Dear Biosleuth." Beyond these notes you will find multiple appendices, including a "Glossary of Terms and Acronyms (including Medical Terminology)," and "Additional Resources for Further Reading" including Internet sites that not only abound in information but also remain current, since they can be regularly updated. I invite you to explore and turn to these additional resources when seeking answers to your own questions, as you continue your journey toward a better understanding of your own situation. I think one of the greatest challenges for patients must be just understanding the lingo that clinicians throw at them. By defining medical terms in ordinary English, we hope to alleviate some of the frustration of a new diagnosis or evolving health condition.

This book is written by a patient, for a patient, and from the patient's perspective. It intentionally and unblushingly explores topics that you will not easily find discussed elsewhere. JoAnne's use of a direct conversational style of writing to share her experiences with the reader, as the "no-holds barred" type of person she is, is one of the qualities that endears her to me, and has made my collaboration on this project so enjoyable. A Neurogenic Bladder is a very personal condition, and discussion can be difficult and embarrassing. The straightforward style that JoAnne employs quickly bypasses the blush factor and gets right to facts and helpful information for coping better during difficult circumstances. We are not medical professionals; ideas presented in this book are not meant to replace medical opinion or care standards but to inform and prepare you to ask the right questions. Not only will you be better prepared to talk to your doctor; we want you never to be afraid to ask for a second opinion. This book is designed to be a source of encouragement and empowerment both to patients and their families. We also hope that members of the medical community will better understand what some of your patients are experiencing. You will find yourself wanting to cheer for JoAnne as you join her on this journey, and she most certainly will be cheering for you! Our wish is that upon learning how she has adapted and re-embraced her life, you too, will find hope and a regained passion for living.

Join me as we learn from one woman's journey.

—Julia Parker, Principal Biosleuth Consulting Services

4. Questions to Consider

Now, Dear Reader, it is your turn. We hope *Beyond Embarrassment* has provided you with new information and, possibly, a different perspective on Neurogenic Bladder and Bowel. Please take a few moments to think about the questions that follow. They have two purposes:

1. To encourage you to think about your previous knowledge and attitudes regarding Neurogenic Bladder and Bowel and any confirmations and changes that may have come from your reading of *Beyond Embarrassment.*
2. To give us, the authors, feedback on how well we have met our goals: education, liberation, and empowerment, and where we all can go from here.

Thank you!

As you start thinking about your answers to these questions, I ask you to consider something. Before I was diagnosed with Neurogenic Bladder and Bowel, I seldom talked about my bladder or bowel except when I was potty training my children. That fear of talking about such issues contributed to years of needless suffering on my part. If I had been more open, especially with my doctors, I would have gotten help sooner. Because of my humiliation and fear of talking about a very basic life activity, I lost opportunities to help countless people struggling with the same thing. Often, if a person does not seek medical help before problems get out of hand, symptoms get worse. Being open and able to have honest conversations can improve your health and that of others.

Now I feel there is no need for people living with Neurogenic Bladder and Bowel to exist in a vacuum and, if I can help someone, then allow me to put my pride aside, and let's talk. As you think about these questions, remember that your friend or neighbor might be struggling with an ill husband who is incontinent and has no idea where to turn because neither has dealt with it before. Remember that this is a normal occurrence and that we all have issues at times.

—JoAnne

Reflections

1. Do certain parts of this book make you feel uncomfortable? Which ones? Why?
2. Did you find parts surprising or shocking? Which ones? Why did they surprise or shock you?
3. Have you ever had a big secret? How did you feel if and when others found out? What were some of their positive and negative responses?
4. Have you ever had a situation in your life when you knew something was physically wrong with you but no one believed you or thought you were making a big deal about nothing? How did you feel? What did you do? How did you overcome that challenging situation? Or did you?

5. At any time, have you struggled with physical or emotional challenges that you thought of as unspeakable or insurmountable? What were they? How did you cope with them? Or did you? Has this book helped you break down barriers that you once thought of as impossible to deal with? What were they? Are you still working on dealing with some? Which ones?
6. Have you had the opportunity to give friends and family acceptance and unconditional support despite all their bumps and warts? Have others done the same for you?
7. Now that you have read *Beyond Embarrassment,* what do you think is the author's most important message? Is it meaningful for you? Why do you think she wrote this book? What is she trying to say?
8. Has this book spiked your interest in bowel and bladder issues? Has it made it easier for you to talk about them? If so, why do you feel more interested or more comfortable talking about it now? If not, why not?
9. What did you expect when you decided to read this book? Has it fulfilled your expectations? What have you learned?
10. Would you recommend this book to others? Why or why not?

Appendices

Absorbency Products on the Market for Incontinence
List compiled by Scott Beckert, RN

Babies/Toddlers:

- Baby Diapers
- Cleansers/Odor Protection
- Creams and Ointments
- Pediatric Diapers/Training Pants
- Washcloths

Bedwetting:

- Adult Briefs
- Baby Diapers
- Cleansers/Odor Protection
- Creams and Ointments
- Disposable Underpads
- Pads/Liners
- Pediatric Diapers/Training Pants
- Protective Underwear/Pull-Ups
- Reusable Underpads

Special Needs:

- Adult Briefs
- Bariatric Briefs
- Cleansers/Odor Protection
- Creams and Ointments
- Disposable Underpads
- Pediatric Diapers/Training Pants
- Protective Underwear/Pull-Ups
- Reusable Chair Pads
- Reusable Underpads

Handicapped:

- Adult Briefs
- Bariatric Briefs
- Cleansers/Odor Protection
- Creams and Ointments
- Disposable Underpads
- Protective Underwear/Pull-Ups
- Reusable Chair Pads
- Reusable Underpads
- Swim Briefs for Adults and Teens

Young Women:

- Bladder Control Pads
- Cleansers/Odor Protection
- Creams and Ointments
- Feminine Hygiene Products
- Pads/Liners
- Protective Underwear/Pull-Ups

Women: Unexpected Leakage:

- Bladder Control Pads
- Cleansers/Odor Protection
- Creams and Ointments
- Pads/Liners
- Protective Underwear/Pull-Ups

Heavy Incontinence:

- Adult Briefs
- Bladder Control Pads
- Cleansers/Odor Protection
- Creams and Ointments
- Disposable Underpads
- Reusable underpads

Men:

- Adult Briefs
- Cleansers/Odor Protection
- Creams and Ointments
- Male Urine Guards
- Protective Underwear/Pull-Ups

Hard To Fit/Bariatric:

- Adult Briefs
- Bariatric Briefs
- Cleansers/Odor Protection
- Creams and Ointments
- Disposable Underpads
- Pads/Liners
- Reusable Chair Pads
- Reusable Underpads

Pets:

- Underpads

Hunter / Sportsman:

- Adult Briefs
- Bladder Control Pads
- Cleansers/Odor Protection
- Disposable Underpads
- Gloves
- Washcloths

*Glossary of Terms & Acronyms**

Adrenal Glands – a pair of glands located by each kidney that secrete hormones: steroids and neurotransmitters; also called suprarenal glands.

Aldosterone – a hormone secreted by the adrenal glands that regulates electrolyte balance by increasing the ability of the kidneys to retain sodium and excrete potassium, which affects blood volume, blood pressure, and water retention.

Ankylosing spondylitis (also called rheumatoid spondylitis or Marie-Strümpell disease) – arthritis of the joints of the spine; it often runs in families.

Antioxidants – substances that protect the body from the harmful effects of oxidation caused by highly reactive substances such as free radicals, by binding or converting them into innate, harmless compounds. They help protect the body at the cellular level from the stress of oxidation.

Atonic bladder – an enlarged bladder that cannot empty/contract because of either a blockage or neurologic abnormalities. Also called Flaccid Bladder.

Adult stem cells – immature cells harvested from adults that mature into the cell type of the environment into which they are placed.

Autologous stem cells – immature cells derived from one's own body that have the potential to mature into different cell types.

Behçet's Disease (also called Behçet's Syndrome) – an inflammatory disease of multiple organ systems especially of the vascular system, in men, the cause of which is unknown. It is rare in the United States, but common in Japan, and the Middle East.

Bladder augmentation – surgical enlargement of the bladder, often removing sections that are scarred, inflamed, or ulcerated.

Bladder Biofeedback – the placement of an electrical patch over the bladder and urethral muscles, connected to a TV screen, to help a patient monitor when muscles contract and learn the sensations of contraction and regain control of the bladder, especially related to stress incontinence and urge incontinence.

Bladder exstrophy repair – the surgery to repair a birth defect in which the bladder is inside-out and sticks out of the abdominal wall. The pelvic bones are also separated. *http://www.nlm.nih.gov/medlineplus/ency/article/002997.htm*

Bladder instillation (also called a bladder wash or bath) – filling the bladder with a sterile liquid solution that is held for varying periods of time, averaging ten to fifteen minutes, before being emptied. It is sometimes used as a treatment for bladder-pain syndrome.

Bladder neck – the base of the bladder, where it joins the urethra.

Bladder Pain Syndrome – formerly known as Interstitial Cystitis.

Bladder stone (Urinary Bladder Calculi) – Stone found in the urinary bladder formed by crystallization and concretion of salts from the urine, usually in stagnant urine, and containing phosphate and oxalate salts of calcium or ammonium. Stones typically form after bacterial colonies start living in the urine, for example, when an indwelling catheter is present or bladder emptying is incomplete; also known as vesicle calculi, bladder stones, or cystoliths.

Bladder Stress test – bearing down or coughing with a full bladder to determine if it leads to leakage of urine.

Brain Fog – the absence of clear thought; to be caught in a mental haze.

Calcium Oxalate Calculus – formed by the accumulation of excess mineral salts in the bladder, these stones may be smooth or covered with sharp spines that dig into the epithelium (inner skin) and prevent the flow of urine.

Catheter – a hollow flexible tube that is inserted into a body cavity or blood vessel either to allow the drainage of fluid or to inflate a blocked passageway. A urinary catheter is inserted into the urethra to drain urine from the bladder.

Chronic Progressive Myelopathy – weakness of the lower extremities and progressive difficulty walking, as well as urinary incontinence, caused by viral infection with HTLV-1 virus.

CIC Catheter – "Clean Intermittent Catheter"

Colostomy – a surgical procedure that creates an artificial passage to eliminate solid waste from the colon.

Congenital sacral dysgenesis – A congenital disorder in which there is abnormal fetal development of the sacrum. This can result in major malformation of the lower vertebrae and pelvis, affecting the spinal nerves in the region, with resulting neurological impairment.

Continence – normal function of the bladder for the controlled elimination of urine.

Crohn's Disease – chronic inflammation (swelling and irritation) that can involve any part of the gastrointestinal tract from mouth to anus, but primarily affects the area from the small intestine to the first section of the colon. It is considered a specific type of IBDs (Inflammatory bowel diseases).

Cushing Syndrome/Disease – an overproduction of ACTH (adrenocorticotropic hormone), a hormone which is accompanied by weakened muscles and often obesity.

Cystectomy – Surgical removal of all or part of the urinary bladder.

Cystoliths – Bladder stones.

Cystometric capacity – Volume of urine that can be held in the bladder.

Cytoscope – a thin tube that contains a camera to allow visual inspection of the inside of the bladder. The images can help determine if there are bladder stones, signs of cancer, unusual swelling of the bladder lining, or bleeding (ulcers).

Detrusor muscle – (muscularis propria of the urinary bladder) contracts when urinating to squeeze out urine.

Detrusor overactivity – is the presence of involuntary detrusor contractions or bladder spasms seen during the filling phase of a urodynamic study.

Dipstick – disposable diagnostic test kit that allows you to determine if you have a urinary tract infection, even at home, especially for people who have chronic urinary tract infections.

Dyssynergia (Detrusor-external sphincter dyssynergia) – lack of coordination such as can occur in Neurogenic Bladder between the coordination of muscles in the bladder wall and sphincter muscles that control the exit of urine through the urethra.

Electromyography (EMG) – the measurement of electrical activity in the bladder neck.

Embryonic stem cell therapy – treatment with immature cells derived from embryos that are versatile enough to convert into specialized cells of a desired type.

Essential nutrients – required for normal functioning but cannot be synthesized by the body; they must be acquired through diet.

Etiology – the cause of a disease, determined by a medical diagnosis, which includes determining what factors might have led to susceptibility.

Foley Catheter – Also known as the suprapubic catheter.

Flaccid bladder – see Atonic Bladder.

Functional Incontinence – the presence of conditions that prevent a person to make it to the toilet, such as a wheelchair constriction or Alzheimer's disease.

Glutathione – the body's primary natural antioxidant and detoxifier.

Heavy Metals – lead, mercury, silver, zinc, copper, aluminum, arsenic, cadmium, iron; metallic compounds that have been linked to disorders of the immune and neurological systems and kidneys.

Inflammatory bowel disease IBD – chronic inflammation of the colon (large intestine) and/or rectum that results in abnormal stools (constipation, diarrhea); anemia, bleeding, weight loss, and/or fever occur in some individuals. Patients with severe symptoms may elect an ileostomy, a surgical bypass of the large intestine (bowel) to relieve long-term suffering.

HTLV-1 Associated Myelopathy (HAM) – a chronic infectious disease affecting the nervous system of those infected with HTLV-1 virus, characterized by progressive difficulty in walking and weakness of the lower extremities, and urinary incontinence, with no evidence of spinal compression or motor-neuron involvement.

Hydronephrosis – swelling within the kidneys, caused by obstruction of any part of the urinary tract, even intermittent, and can lead to distention of the renal system.

Hydroureter – swelling of the ureter.

Induced pluripotent stem cells (iPS) – adult stem cells that have been genetically modified to act more like embryonic stem cells.

Interstitial Cystitis – now known as Bladder Pain Syndrome.

Ipsilateral – occurring or affecting the same side of the body.

Irritable Bowel Syndrome (IBS) – is a sometimes painful syndrome of the gastrointestinal tract with similar symptoms to IBD (constipation, diarrhea); the colon does not show signs of inflammation or sores (ulcers) upon examination. It is sometimes referred to as nervous colon or spastic bowel or colon.

Marfan Syndrome – a rare disease of the connective tissue, most commonly associated with unusual height/length of limbs.

Meningomyelitis – an inflamed spinal cord, often involving the surrounding membranes.

Mesenchymal stromal stem cells (MSCs) – a stem cell within connective tissue that can produce connective tissue including fat, muscle, bone, and cartilage.

Micturition – urination.

MTHFR (Methylenetetrahydrofolate Reductase) gene – encodes an enzyme critical in the production of methionine, one of the essential amino acids involved in normal metabolism in the body.

Multiple Sclerosis (MS) – a chronic autoimmune disorder which destroys the protective myelin sheath that insulates nerve fibers in the central nervous system. MS leads to weakness of muscles and loss of balance and coordination, and can eventually affect bodily functions, including control of the bladder and bowel.

Multipotent cells – immature cells that carry the potential to convert into seemingly unrelated cell types. These cells are found in adult adipose tissue (fat), cardiac tissue (heart), and bone marrow.

Neurogenic Bladder – bladder dysfunction due to interference with the normal nerve pathways that control urination.

Neuro-modulation – electrical stimulation of the nerves that control the bladder using a device placed outside the body or implanted surgically.

Nerve Growth Factor (NGF) – a protein that controls the growth of both sensory and sympathetic nerves.

Nocturia – excessive urination occurring at night.

Obstructive uropathy – an obstruction of the urethra that blocks the flow of urine, causing retention or incomplete emptying of the bladder.

Omentum – a fatty tissue lying above the stomach, containing stem cells.

Overactive bladder – an increased frequency of urination, with or without urge incontinence, often the result of involuntary bladder-muscle contractions.

Overflow Incontinence – uncontrollable leakage of urine as a result of great pressure on the urethra from an overfilled bladder.

Paraparesis – a partial paralysis of the lower extremities.

Paresis – partial or incomplete paralysis.

Paresthesia – an abnormal subjective sensation such as burning, prickling, tingling, or numbness that can vary according to circumstances, including positional changes.

Paruresis (Shy Bladder) – known also as bashful bladder or urophobia: the inability to urinate in the presence of others.

Pessary– a stiff ring used to treat stress incontinence; it is inserted into the vagina against the urethra to help reposition the urethra and reduce potential stress that could cause leakage of urine.

Proanthocyanidins – chemical component in cranberries that helps prevent bacteria from attaching to membranes.

Probiotic – a dairy supplement containing a live culture of the beneficial organism, Lactobacillus acidophilus, to improve digestion, fight bacterial infections of the urinary tract, and promote gastrointestinal health and general well-being.

Profilometry – a method to study bladder disorders using the internal pressure of the urethra and electromyography (EMG).

PVC – Polyvinyl chloride.

PVP (Polyvinyl pyrolidone) – the material used in the surface of CIC catheters. (When the CIC catheter is submersed in water, the PVP absorbs it and creates a smooth, slippery surface that is isotonic, which means it is the same salt concentration as urine.)

Pyelonephritis – inflammation of the kidney (upper urinary tract), usually following cystitis/infection of the bladder.

Renal calculi – Stones in the kidney (kidney stones), usually formed in the urine-collecting area of the kidney (kidney pelvis). Their sizes vary, and most contain calcium oxalate.

Renal Failure – malfunction or loss of kidney function, resulting in the inability to filter waste products from the blood.

Rhabdosphincter – a sphincter made of striated muscle.

Sacral agenesis – A condition that exists when either part or all of the sacrum is absent. It is usually associated with impaired development of sacral spinal nerves and with consequent pelvic organ and lower-limb dysfunction.

Sacral Foramen – openings in the sacrum that allow the sacral nerves to gain access to the pelvic organs that they enervate.

Sacral Nerve – any of five pairs of spinal nerves that control function of the bladder, bowel, and other pelvic functions; it passes through the sacral foramen.

Sacrum – the name of the end of the spinal column, composed of five fused vertebrae; the terminal end of the sacrum is known as the coccyx.

SCI – acronym for Spinal Cord Injury.

Scoliosis – abnormal curvature of the spine to the side.

Sling surgery – utilizing a mesh to lift the bladder and urethra to help regain bladder control.

Spastic bladder – see Detrusor overactivity

Sphincter – a circular band of muscle that constricts and relaxes to allow passage or provide a seal between organs or at an orifice to the outside of the body.

Spina bifida – A condition in which the bones of the spine do not close. In cases of "myelomeningocoele," the bony abnormality is accompanied by abnormal development of the spinal cord or nerves and their covering membranes, which leads to abnormalities in the nerve supply to the lower limbs and pelvic organs.

Stoma – Creation of an opening in which urine flows into a special pouch (also referred to as urinary diversion), especially after a bladder removal (cystectomy). Urine empties through the stoma into either a bag outside the body or into a pouch inside the abdomen. At intervals throughout the day, the patient puts a catheter into the stoma and empties the pouch. Patients with either type of urostomy must be very careful to keep the area in and around the stoma clean to prevent infection. Serious potential complications may include kidney infection and small-bowel obstruction. http://kidney.niddk.nih.gov/kudiseases/pubs/interstitialcystitis/#treatments

Stress incontinence (SUI) – the sudden involuntary release of urine caused by a muscle strain in the pelvis following laughing, sneezing, coughing, or exercise. Common in women who have weakened pelvic muscles, as a result of childbirth.

Submucosa – the loose layer of tissue lying beneath a mucosal membrane; contains blood vessels and connective tissue.

Suprapubic – above the pubic bone.

Suprapubic Catheterization – an indwelling catheter, such as the Foley catheter popular in many hospitals for patients confined to a bed.

Tethered Cord Syndrome – a birth defect involving the spinal cord during development which may contribute to incontinence, especially a spastic, low-capacity bladder, pain in the lower extremities in some cases and possibly scoliosis.

Transient incontinence – leakage of urine that is connected to an illness or medical condition (pregnancy) which is corrected when the condition is removed.

Tropical Spastic Paraparesis (TSP) – see HTLV-1 Associated Myelopathy (HAM).

UPEC (Uropathogenic Escherichia coli) – most common bacteria that have specific factors that aid their ability to infect the urinary tract and lead to urinary tract infections.

Ureter – tubes that connect both kidneys to the bladder; they channel the flow of urine as it exits the body.

Urgency incontinence (spastic paralysis or urge incontinence) – the sudden unexpected strong urge to urinate that results in leakage of urine such as during sleep or brought on by sensory triggers, including visual, auditory, or even the act of touching running water.

Urinary incontinence – loss of bladder control or "Urinary leakage."

Urinary Tract – organs of your body involved in the production and elimination of urine: kidneys, ureters, bladder, and urethra.

Urinary Tract Infection (UTI) – presence of infectious germs (bacteria) in the urine.

Urodynamics Tests – a useful panel of diagnostic tests used to determine Neurogenic Bladder type. These tests utilize a thin tube, which is placed in the bladder, disclose the exact parameters of lower urinary tract function, and help determine pressure within the cavity of the bladder muscle.

Urosepsis – bacterial infection in the bloodstream caused by the absorption of infected urine from a severe urinary tract infection.

Urothelial carcinoma (Transitional cell carcinoma (TCC) – a malignant cancer derived of the mucous membrane, primarily in the bladder and ureters, which can increase internal pressures within the kidneys and damage them.

Urostomy – a surgical procedure that creates an artificial passage to eliminate urine from the body.

Vesico-ureteral reflux – an abnormal reverse backflow of urine into the ureter(s) from the bladder.

Vesicovaginal – anything that relates to the bladder and vagina.

Wolfram Syndrome – a debilitating autosomal recessive genetic disorder that is often referred to by an acronym of symptoms that develop, "DIDMOAD" (diabetes insipidus, diabetes mellitus, optic atrophy and deafness).

*Many of these entries are adapted from the *Clinical Glossary on PubMed Health* http://www.ncbi.nlm.nih.gov/pubmedhealth/PMH0055298/

Additional Resources for Further Reading

Neurogenic Bladder:

PubMedHealth – For Consumers

http://www.ncbi.nlm.nih.gov/pubmedhealth/?term=Neurogenic+Bladder&filters=

To Learn More . . .

We hope you have found this book to be a great encouragement and source for better understanding the many health issues that can affect the bladder. An editor in the publishing industry once explained to me that every book has potential value and insight, since no two authors who write on the same subject will ever duplicate each

Knowledge Nugget:

Amazon is a great source of information on the current status of a book (including if new editions have been published). Most public libraries will borrow any book you wish through an Interlibrary Loan (ILL). Consult your library for specific policies.

other. It's just not going to happen.

The following are additional sources for you to consider. They were available and relevant at the time of this publication.

Knowledge Nugget:

Of course, you may wish to consult with a medical librarian to get started on your search for health information. Hospitals and their medical libraries were originally maintained exclusively for the use of their physicians and staff. Now, many community hospitals include a Consumer Library, which is open to the public, with its specialized medical information that you won't find in most city or county public libraries. If you are fortunate to live near a university with a medical school, you should check with them to see if they are open to the public for reference services.

Recommended Books — To Learn More:

1. Beyer, Julie, MA, RD. *Confident Choices: A Cookbook for Interstitial Cystitis and Overactive Bladder.* NutraConsults, LLC, 2009.
2. Gartley, Cheryle B., Mary Radtke Klein, Christine Norton, Anita Saltmarche. *Managing Life with Incontinence.* The Simon Foundation, 2012.
3. Houser, Elizabeth E. and Stephanie Riley Hahn. *A Woman's Guide to Pelvic Health: Expert Advice for Women of All Ages,* Baltimore: Johns Hopkins University Press, 2012.
4. *Johns Hopkins Health Book,* "A guide to urinary incontinence," Baltimore MD: Johns Hopkins University Press, 2008.
5. Kassai, Kathryn PT, CES, Perelli, Kim. *The Bathroom Key,* New York: Demos Health,, 2012.
6. Kavaler, Elizabeth. *A Seat on the Aisle, Please,* Springer Science+Business , New York, NY: Copernicus Books, 2006.
7. Larsen, Laura, ed. *Women's Health Concerns Sourcebook,* 4th ed., Detroit, MI: Omnigraphics, Inc., [2013].
8. Roberts, Val. *Coping With an Overactive Bladder: A Guide for Women Suffering from Urgency and Related Bladder Problems* [Kindle Edition]. Phrase Publishing Ltd, 2012.

Exercise Video:

Hab It: Pelvic Floor.

Tasha Mulligan (Actor), PT Partners, LLC | Format: DVD (2008).

More than 20 million women suffer from the consequences of weakened pelvic-floor muscles, which can lead to incontinence or prolapse. Whether you are a new mom or a serious athlete, young or old, the symptoms of pelvic-floor weakness can cause embarrassment and stop you from doing the activities you love.

Note: Video includes excellent informational segment and then exercise segments, divided into four different workouts.

Recommended Websites and Blogs

"Bladder," PubMed Health Information, http://www.ncbi.nlm.nih.gov/pubmedhealth/PMHT0021898/

Continence Promotion Committee (International Consultation on Incontinence), http://www.ics.org/ViewCommittee.aspx?ViewCommitteeID=3

Diagrams and explanations of types of bladder disease and treatments

http://kidney.niddk.nih.gov/KUDiseases/pubs/bcw_ez/index.aspx#

http://kidney.niddk.nih.gov/KUDiseases/pubs/nervedisease/index.aspx

Digestive Diseases A-Z, accessed 08/29/2015, http://www.niddk.nih.gov/health-information/health-topics/digestive-diseases/Pages/default.aspx

The Free Dictionary Medical Dictionary by Farlex, accessed April 7, 2015, http://medical-dictionary.thefreedictionary.com/.

Glossary from the National Association for Continence (NAFC), accessed April 9, 2015, http://www.nafc.org/glossary.

Drugs, Supplements, and Herbal Information, http://www.nlm.nih.gov/medlineplus/druginfo.

Inserting an intermittent urinary catheter

"Self-catheterization – female," MedlinePlus, accessed April 10, 2015, http://www.nlm.nih.gov/medlineplus/ency/patientinstructions/000144.htm.

Nall, Rachel, "Clean Intermittent Self-Catheterization," posted August 7, 2012, accessed April 10, 2015, http://www.healthline.com/health/clean-intermittent-self-catheterization#Overview1.ipe.

"Neurogenic Bladder" (a MedlinePlus Article), http://www.nlm.nih.gov/medlineplus/ency/article/000754.htm.

"Urinary bladder," *Wikipedia,* last modified March 7, 2015, http://en.wikipedia.org/wiki/Urinary_bladder.

"Urinary incontinence fact sheet," US Department of Health and Human Services Office on Women's Health, accessed July 13, 2015, http://www.womenshealth.gov/publications/our-publications/fact-sheet/urinary-incontinence.html?from=AtoZ.

"Urinary System," *Wikipedia,* accessed April 9, 2015, http://en.wikipedia.org/wiki/Urinary_System – A nice overview of the Urinary/Renal system with links to each of the organs, including the bladder.

University of Washington Urological Information, http://sci.washington.edu/info/pamphlets/bladder.asp

Patient-Support Forums

1. Inspire
2. "Patients Like Me: Live Better, Together!" A patient network for sharing treatment experiences, accessed April 7, 2015, http://www.patientslikeme.com.
3. YourKidneys.com by DaVita, a community resource for information on kidney disease, accessed April 7, 2015, http://www.yourkidneys.com.

Useful Blogs:

Trudy Triumph – a Blog About Neurogenic Bladder and Bowel: http://www.trudytriumph.com.

Dr. Jill – Your Functional Medicine Expert: http://www.jillcarnahan.com/dr-jills-blog/.

PubMed Health – Current systematic reviews related to Neurogenic Bladder (updated medical knowledge and clinical standards regarding published evidence about incidence, risk factors, and management options for Neurogenic Bladder*):

http://www.ncbi.nlm.nih.gov/pubmedhealth/?term=Neurogenic+Bladder

**Select "Save Search" to complete the form and receive direct notifications by e-mail of any changes or new articles added on the topic to the PubMed Health database.*

Additional Organizations/Nonprofits That Provide Reliable Health Information:

American Association of Health and Disability
110 N Washington St.
Suite 328-J
Rockville MD 20850

American Urogynecologic Society
2025 M Street NW
Suite 800
Washington DC 20036

American Urological Association Foundation
Website: www.urologyhealth.org
E-mail: info@urologycarefoundation.org

National Center for Complementary and Alternative Medicine (NCCAM)
Website: www.nccam.nih.gov

National Institute on Aging (NIA)
Website: www.nia.nih.gov

National Kidney and Urologic Diseases Information Clearinghouse
Website: www.kidney.niddk.nih.gov
E-mail: nkudic@info.niddk.nih.gov

National Women's Health Resource Center
Website: www.healthywomen.org
E-mail: info@healthywomen.org

Office of Women's Health, Centers for Disease Control and Prevention (CDC)

Website: www.cdc.gov/women

E-mail: cdcinfo@cdc.gov

Office on Women's Health, US Department of Health and Human Services (HHS)

Website: www.womenshealth.gov

Society for Women's Health Research

Website: www.womenshealthresearch.org

Society of Urologic Nurses

SUNA Headquarters

East Holy Ave. Box 56

Pitman, NJ 08071-0056

Website: https://www.suna.org/

Under Active Bladder Foundation

PO Box 5080

6360 Broad Street

Pittsburgh, PA 15206-9998

Website: http://www.underactivebladder.org/

Weight-Control Information Network (WIN)

Website: www.win.niddk.nih.gov

E-mail: win@info.niddk.nih.gov

References and Notes (by chapter):

Part 1: My Story

1. Diagnosis: Neurogenic Bladder

Quotation –

1. Gardner, John W, "John W. Gardner Quotes & Sayings," accessed March 12, 2014, bit.ly/1Cn4HVm.

2. Attitude Check – How Did This Happen to Me?

1. Buechner, Frederick, "Quotes from Frederick Buechner," accessed April 9, 2015, https://www.goodreads.com/quotes/134865-you-can-kiss-your-family-and-friends-good-bye-and-put.

Vaginal Delivery

2. Glazener CM, MacArthur C, Hagen S, Elders A, Lancashire R, Herbison GP, Wilson PD; ProLong Study Group. "Twelve-year follow-up of conservative management of postnatal urinary and fecal incontinence and prolapse outcomes: randomized controlled trial," *BJOG*. 121, no. 1 (2014 Jan): 112-20. Epub 2013 Oct 22. PubMed PMID: 24148807. doi: 10.1111/1471-0528.12473.

Surgical Trauma

Vaginal Hysterectomy

3. Genadry, Rene MD, and Jacek L. Mostwin, MD. *A Woman's Guide to Urinary Incontinence*. Johns Hopkins Press, 2008

4. Iwanowicz-Palus GJ, Stadnicka G, Włoszczak-Szubzda A., "Medical and psychosocial factors conditioning development of stress urinary incontinence (SUI)," *Ann Agric Environ Med.*; 20, no. 1 (2013): 135-9. PubMed PMID: 23540227.

5. Rackley, Raymond R, MD; Chief Editor: Edward David Kim, MD, FACS, "Neurogenic Bladder," Medscape eMedicine Drugs & Diseases article, last modified December 6, 2013, http://emedicine.medscape.com/article/453539-overview#aw2aab6b5. The percentage of Neurogenic Bladders among incontinent children ages twelve and younger was much lower, at 2.9 percent, compared to 9.9 percent of patients with incontinence of twenty years or greater; the mean age in those with Neurogenic Bladder was 62.5 years, and they were 60 percent female.

3. Bowel Journey from Symptoms to Survival

"Who Designed The Human Body? – Engineers' Perspective," accessed April 9, 2015, http://www.gotjokes.net/engineering-jokes/engineering-jokes/human-body-design.html

4. Bladder Infections: Signs & Solutions

1. Excerpted from "Urinary Tract Infections Fact Sheet," US Department of Health and Human Services Office on Women's Health, accessed, May 23, 2015, http://www.womenshealth.gov.

Prevention

2. Rossi R, Porta S, Canovi B. "Overview on cranberry and urinary tract infections in females," *J Clin Gastroenterology* 44 Suppl 1 (2010 Sep): S61-2. Review. PubMed PMID: 20495471. doi:10.1097/MCG.0b013e3181d2dc8e.

Bladder Pain Syndrome

3. Larsen, Laura, ed. "Urinary Tract Disorders," in *Women's Health Concerns Sourcebook,* 4th ed., Detroit, MI:, Omnigraphics, Inc., [2013].

4. Hanno P, Lin A, Nordling J, Nyberg L, van Ophoven A, Ueda T, Wein A, "Bladder Pain Syndrome Committee of the International Consultation on Incontinence," Bladder Pain Syndrome Committee of the International Consultation on Incontinence. *Neurourol Urodyn.* 29, no. 1 (2010): 191-8. Review. PubMed PMID: 20025029. doi: 10.1002/nau.20847.

5. Painful Bladder Syndrome (IC), Chapter 58.1 Originally excerpted from "Interstitial Cystitis/Bladder Pain Syndrome Fact Sheet," US Department of Health and Human Services Office on Women's Health (www.womenshealth.gov), pg 631-637.

6. "Interstitial Cystitis/Painful Bladder Syndrome," National Institute of Diabetes and Digestive and Kidney Diseases (NIDDK), National Institutes of Health (NIH), last modified September 10, 2013, http://kidney.niddk.nih.gov/kudiseases/pubs/interstitialcystitis/#.

Kidneys

7. "Top 15 Healthy Foods for People with Kidney Disease," accessed May 23, 2015, http://www.davita.com/kidney-disease/diet-and-nutrition/lifestyle/top-15-healthy-foods-for-people-with-kidney-disease/e/5347.

8. "10 Antioxidant Foods for the Kidney Diet," accessed May 23, 2015, http://www.davita.com/kidney-disease/diet-and-nutrition/diet-basics/10-antioxidant-foods-for-the-kidney-diet/e/7084.

9. "Dialysis: It's a Lifesaver," accessed May 23, 2015, http://www.davita.com/kidney-disease/dialysis.

5. Intimacy

1. "Health Benefits of the Female Orgasm," Holly Franklin, last modified January 22, 2009, accessed April 8, 2015, bit.ly/1c9Tz86.

6. Conquest over Depression

1. "Depression: What Is Depression? What are the signs and symptoms of depression? and How is depression diagnosed and treated?" The National Institute of Mental Health (NIMH), Transforming the understanding and treatment of mental illnesses, part of the National Institutes of Health (NIH), a component of the US Department of Health and Human Services, accessed April 8, 2015, http://www.nimh.nih.gov/health/publications/depression/index.shtml.

2. Kreder K. and Dmochowski, R., ed. *The Overactive Bladder,* Boca Raton: CRC Press 2007.

The Importance of Research

3. Oh SJ, Shin HI, Paik NJ, Yoo T, Ku JH. Depressive symptoms of patients using clean intermittent catheterization for Neurogenic Bladder secondary to spinal cord injury. *Spinal Cord.* 2006 Dec. 44(12):757-62. PubMed PMID: 16432529. doi:10.1038/sj.sc.3101903; published online 24 January 2006 http://www.nature.com/sc/journal/v44/n12/pdf/3101903a.pdf

NOTE: Spinal Cord is published by the Nature Publishing Group, (one of the most prestigious and influential scientific and medical-research publishers in the world).

7. A Frank and Honest Look at Devices and Aids

1. Mandela, Nelson, Nelson, R., ed. May 27, 2014, accessed April 9, 2015, http://quoteinvestigator.com/category/nelson-mandela/.

2. "What is Urinary Incontinence?" accessed April 9, 2015, http://www.sharecare.com/health/urinary-incontinence.

Incontinence Pads and Diapers

3. National Association for Continence (NAFC), accessed April 9, 2015, www.nafc.org/demand-to-be-dry.

4. "Incontinence Solutions / Resources," Simon Foundation for Continence, accessed April 9, 2015, http://www.simonfoundation.org/Incontinence_Solutions.html.

5. Darkow T, Fontes CL, Williamson TE., "Costs associated with the management of overactive bladder and related comorbidities," *Pharmacotherapy* 25, no. 4 (2005 Apr): 511-9. PubMed PMID: 15977912.

6. Foxman B. "Epidemiology of urinary tract infections: incidence, morbidity, and economic costs," *Dis Mon.* 49 (2003):53-70. doi: http://dx.doi.org/10.1016/S0011-5029(03)90000-9.

7. Ganz ML, Smalarz AM, Krupski TL, Anger JT, Hu JC, Wittrup-Jensen KU, Pashos CL. Economic costs of overactive bladder in the United States. *Urology* 75, no. 3 (2010 Mar): 526-32, 532.e1-18. PubMed PMID: 20035977. doi:10.1016/j.urology.2009.06.096.

Catheters

8. Spinu, A., *et al.*, "Intermittent catheterization. Neurogenic Bladder can also have a pharmacological or psychological basis," *J. Medicine and Life* 5, no. 1 (2012): 21-28.

The use of Clean Intermittent Catheterization is so well accepted in some parts of the world that they are provided for free by the health agencies of many countries. They are viewed as an application of the concept of the inseparability of biomedical and social aspects in human functioning, based on the system established by the World Health Organization in 2001, the International Classification of Functioning, Disabilities and Health (ICFCH). For example, since 2008, the Romanian National Assurance House (the Health Plan of Romania) has fully supported the unlimited use of four closed-circuit hydrophilic catheters per day for patients diagnosed with Neurogenic Bladder.

9. De Ridder DJMK, Everaert K, Garcia Fernandez L, *et al.* Intermittent catheterization with hydophilic-coated catheters reduces the risk of clinical urinary tract infections in spinal-cord injured patients: a prospective, randomized, parallel comparative trial. Europ. Urology 2005 48: 991-995.

10. Vapnek JM, Maynard FM, Kim J., "A prospective randomized trial of the LoFric hydrophilic-coated catheter versus conventional plastic catheter for clean intermittent catheterization," *Journal of Urology* 169 (2003): 994-998.

11. Tenke P, Jackel M, Nagy E. Prevention and treatment of catheter-associated infections: myth or reality? *EAU Update Ser.* 2 (2004): 106-115.

12. Donnellan SM, Bolton DM. "The impact of contemporary bladder management technique on struvite calculi associated with spinal cord injury." BJU International 1999 84(3): 280-285.

History of catheters

13. "Foley catheter," *Wikipedia,* last modified December 17, 2014, http://en.wikipedia.org/wiki/Foley_catheter.

14. "A brief history of urinary catheters," *Urology Today,* http://www.urotoday.com/Urologic-Catheters/a-brief-history-of-urinary-catheters.html.

15. Dixon L, Dolan LM, Brown K, Hilton P, "RCT of urethral versus suprapubic catheterization," *Br J Nurs.*19, no. 18 (2010 Oct 14-27): S7-13.

Foley Catheter

16. Sulzbach, L.M., "Avoiding Indwelling Urinary Catheters," 22, no. 3 (2002): 84-87. http://ccn.aacnjournals.org/content/22/3/84.full.

17. Stickler DJ,, Feneley RCL, "The encrustation and blockage of long-term indwelling bladder catheters: a way forward in prevention and control," *Spinal Cord* 48 (2010): 784-790.

18. Rauscher, M., "Increased bladder cancer risk in spinal cord injury linked with indwelling catheters," *Arch. Phys Med. Rehabil.* 83 (2002): 346-351.

8. Living Life Well

1. Voltaire, "Quotes on Living Well," accessed April 10, 2015, http://www.essentiallifeskills.net/quotes-on-living-well.html.

Eating well

2. Kranjg wellessentiallifeskills.net/quotes-on-living-well.htmlord injury linked with urinary tract infections in women: a randomized clinical trial, *tWorld J Urol.* 32, no. 1 (2014 Feb): 79-84. Epub 2013 Apr 30, PubMed PMID: 23633128. doi:10.1007/s00345-013-1091-6.

Yearly Physicals and Other Medical Care

3. Lukacz ES, Sampselle C, Gray M, Macdiarmid S, Rosenberg M, Ellsworth P, Palmer MH., "A healthy bladder: a consensus statement," *Int J Clin Pract.* 65, no. 10 (2011 Oct): 1026-36. PubMed PMID: 21923844; PubMed Central PMCID: PMC3206217. doi:10.1111/j.1742-1241.2011.02763.x.

4. Interstitial Cystitis Diet, accessed May 23, 2015, http://www.ic-diet.com.

5. Manack A, Motsko SP, Jones JK, Ravelo A, Haag-Molkenteller C, Dmochowski R., "Epidemiology of Neurogenic Bladder Patients in a US Claims Database," American Urology Association Annual Meeting – Moderated Poster Presentation (April 25–30, 2009): Chicago, IL, http://www.deggegroup.com/2009-AUA%20-%20Epi%20of%20NOAB%2056478.pdf

Working

6. "Urinary Incontinence New Hope: Research Activities, No. 383 (July 2012), Agency for Healthcare Research and Quality, Rockville, MD, last modified and archived July 2012, http://archive.ahrq.gov/news/newsletters/research-activities/jul12/0712RA3.html.

7. McKay, Dawn Rosenberg, "Working With a Disability: How the Law Protects Your Rights," accessed April 9, 2015, http://careerplanning.about.com/cs/personalissues/a/disability_act.htm.

Traveling

8. "21 Tip Times to Help You Pack for a Trip," accessed April 9, 2015, http://www.travellerspoint.com/packing-Tip Time.cfm.

Other Resources that Inspired:

Albers, Susan Psy.D., "The 10 Best Healthy Eating Quotes," (Jul 13, 2011), accessed April 9, 2015, http://www.psychologytoday.com/blog/comfort-cravings/201107/the-10-best-healthy-eating-quotes.

Brillat-Savarin, Anthelme, (1755–1826), French gourmet & lawyer, *The Physiology of Taste*, (1825), accessed April 9, 2015, http://www.quotationspage.com/quote/2032.html

Clift, Eleanor, "If you think of life and death on a continuum," bit.ly/1lty13s.

Coville, Bruce, "The real heroes are the librarians and teachers," accessed April 9, 2015, https://www.goodreads.com/quotes/256165-the-real-heroes-are-the-librarians-and-teachers-who-at.

"The IC Food Lists – How To Begin," accessed April 9, 2015, http://www.ic-network.com/patient-resources/diet/diet-introduction/#icfoodlist.

Kinsolver, Barbara, 1955–, American novelist, accessed April 9, 2015, http://www.brainyquote.com/quotes/quotes/b/barbarakin461562.html.

Osborne, Jill, MA, "What's the Worst Drink For IC Ever?," accessed April 9, 2015, http://www.ic-network.com/whats-the-worst-drink-for-ic-ever.

"Quotes About Teachers," accessed April 9, 2015, http://www.goodreads.com/quotes/tag/teachers.

9. Parenting a Child with Bladder Problems

Giving our Children What They Need

1. Lukacz ES, Sampselle C, Gray M, Macdiarmid S, Rosenberg M, Ellsworth P, Palmer MH., "A healthy bladder: a consensus statement," *Int J Clin Pract.* 65, no. 10 (2011 Oct): 1026-36. PubMed PMID: 21923844; PubMed Central PMCID: PMC3206217. doi:10.1111/j.1742-1241.2011.02763.x.

2. Vernon S, Lundblad B, Hellstrom AL., "Children's experiences of school toilets present a risk to their physical and psychological health," *Child Care Health* Dev. 29, no 1 (2003 Jan): 47-53. PubMed PMID: 12534566.

10. Not Broken but Beautiful: Moving Beyond Embarrassment

1. Wall, L. Lewis, "Jesus and the Unclean Woman: How a story in Mark's gospel sheds light on the problem of obstetric fistula," January 13, 2010, last modified January 18, 2010, http://www.christianitytoday.com/ct/2010/january/17.48.html.

2. "What Is a Fistula?" accessed April 9, 2015

3. "Ag Giant Dies, Stidolph, 80, Invented Broccoli Florets and Dumped Veggies on President's Lawn" *Salinas Californian,* (Wednesday April 21 2004): front page.

4. Love Quotes, accessed April 10, 2015, http://www.great-inspirational-quotes.com/love-quotes.html.

PART 2: BLOG CHATTER

I. "Dear Biosleuth" – Questions Posed by Patients and their Families

I. What causes a neurogenic bladder?

1. Manack A, Motsko SP, Jones JK, Ravelo A, Haag-Molkenteller C, Dmochowski R., "Epidemiology of Neurogenic Bladder Patients in a US Claims Database," American Urology Association Annual Meeting – Moderated Poster Presentation (April 25–30, 2009): Chicago, IL, http://www.deggegroup.com/2009-AUA%20-%20Epi%20of%20NOAB%2056478.pdf

2. Heimer, G, and G. Samsioe, "Effects of vaginally delivered estrogens," *Acta Obstet Gynecol Scand Suppl.*163 (1996): 1-2. PubMed PMID: 8916468

3. Long CY, Liu CM, Hsu SC, Chen YH, Wu CH, Tsai EM., "A randomized comparative study of the effects of oral and topical estrogen therapy on the lower urinary tract

of hysterectomized postmenopausal women," *Fertil Steril.* 85, no. 1 (2006 Jan): 155-60. PubMed PMID: 16412747.

4. Blochin EB, Park KJ, Tickoo SK, Reuter VE, Al-Ahmadie H., "Urothelial carcinoma with prominent squamous differentiation in the setting of Neurogenic Bladder: role of human papillomavirus infection," *Mod Pathol.* 25, no. 11 (2012 Nov): 1534-42. (Epub 2012 Jul 6.) PubMed PMID: 22766788. doi:10.1038/modpathol.2012.112.

5. Palleschi G, Pastore AL, Maggioni C, Fuschi A, Pacini L, Petrozza V, Carbone A., "Overactive bladder in diabetes mellitus patients: a questionnaire-based observational investigation," *World J Urol.* 32 no. 4 (2014 Aug):1021-5. PubMed PMID: 24100404. doi: 10.1007/s00345-013-1175-3.

6. Jacobs BL, Smaldone MC, Tyagi V, Philips BJ, Jackman SV, Leng WW, Tyagi P., "Increased nerve growth factor in neurogenic overactive bladder and interstitial cystitis patients," *Can J Urol.*17 no. 1 (2010 Feb): 4989-94. PubMed PMID: 20156378.

7. "Marfan Syndrome Factsheet," accessed April 10, 2015, http://chealth.canoe.ca/condition_info_details.asp?disease_id=250.

8. "My Story – Man with a Neurogenic Bladder due to Marfan's Syndrome," last modified 14 July 2009, http://www.simonfoundation.org/My_Story_Man_Neurogenic_Bladder_Due_Marfans_Syndrome.html.

9. Wolfram syndrome, Genetics Home Reference: Your Guide to Understanding Genetic Conditions, US National Library of Medicine, http://ghr.nlm.nih.gov/condition/wolfram-syndrome.

10. Hall SA, Curto TM, Onyenwenyi A, Lemack GE, Tennstedt SL, Link CL, McKinlay JB., "Characteristics of persons with overactive bladder of presumed neurologic origin: results from the Boston Area Community Health (BACH) survey," *Neurourol Urodyn.*31, no. 7 (2012 Sep): 1149-55. PMID: 22674347; PubMed Central PMCID: PMC3419809. doi:10.1002/nau.22232.

11. Gatti, John M MD; Chief Editor, Marc Cendron, MD. "Ureteral Duplication, Ureteral Ectopia, and Ureterocele," *Medscape,* last modified September 12, 2013, http://emedicine.medscape.com/article/1017202-overview.

12. Puri BK, Shah M, Julu PO, Kingston MC, Monro JA, "Urinary bladder detrusor dysfunction symptoms in lyme disease," *Int Neurourol J.*17, no. 3 (2013 Sep): 127-9. Epub 2013 Sep 30. PubMed PMID: 24143291; Central PMCID: PMC3797892 doi:10.5213/inj.2013.17.3.127.

13. "Neurosyphilis," accessed April 10, 2015, http://www.medmerits.com/index.php/article/neurosyphilis/P2.

14. Campos-Sousa RN, Quagliato EM, Almeida KJ, Castro IA, Campelo V., "Urinary dysfunction with detrusor hyperactivity in women with Parkinson's disease cannot be blamed as a factor of worsening motor performance," *Arq Neuropsiquiatr.*71, no. 9A (2013 Sep): 591-5. PubMed PMID: 24141437. doi:10.1590/0004-282X20130101.

15. Mink PJ, Alexander DD, Barraj LM, Kelsh MA, Tsuji JS., "Low-level arsenic exposure in drinking water and bladder cancer: A review and meta-analysis," *Regul Toxicol Pharmacol.* 52, no. 3 (2008 Dec): 299-310. Epub 2008 Aug 26. Review. PMID: 18783726. doi:10.1016/j.yrtph.2008.08.010.

16. Fowles J, Dybing E., "Application of toxicological risk assessment principles to the chemical constituents of cigarette smoke," *Tob Control* 12, no. 4 (2003 Dec): 424-30. PMID: 14660781 PMC: 1747794. doi:10.1136/tc.12.4.424.

17. Larsen, Laura, ed. "Urinary Tract Disorders," in *Women's Health Concerns Sourcebook*, 4th ed., Detroit, MI:, Omnigraphics, Inc., [2013].

18. Handa VL, Blomquist JL, McDermott KC, Friedman S, Muñoz A., "Pelvic floor disorders after vaginal birth: effect of episiotomy, perineal laceration, and operative birth," *Obstet Gynecol.*119 no. 2, Pt. 1 (2012 Feb): 233-9. PubMed PMID: 22227639; PubMed Central PMCID: PMC3266992. doi:10.1097/AOG.0b013e318240df4f.

19. Chartier-Kastler E, Ayoub N, Mozer P, Richard F, Ruffion A., "[Neurourological consequences of stress urinary incontinence and pelvic repair surgery]," *Prog Urol.*17, no. 3 (2007 May): 385-92. Review. French. PubMed PMID: 17622064.

20. Spinu, A., et al., "Intermittent catheterization. Neurogenic Bladder can also have a pharmacological or psychological basis," *J. Medicine and Life* 5, no. 1 (2012): 21-28.

II. What typical tests and procedures are performed in the urologist's office?

1. "Urodynamic testing," *Wikipedia,* last modified February 4, 2015, http://en.wikipedia.org/wiki/Urodynamic_testing.

2. Benninghoff, A. Function (Physiology) of the Bladder Filling and Micturition, http://www.urology-textbook.com/bladder-function.html, accessed May 23, 2015.

3. Truzzi JC, Almeida FM, Nunes EC, Sadi MV, "Residual urinary volume and urinary tract infection – when are they linked?," J Urol. 180 no. 1 (2008 Jul):182-5. PubMed PMID: 18499191. doi: 10.1016/j.juro.2008.03.044.

4. Larsen, Laura, ed. "Urinary Tract Disorders," in *Women's Health Concerns Sourcebook,* 4th ed., Detroit, MI:, Omnigraphics, Inc., [2013].

III. Do cranberry products help prevent bladder infections?

1. "Urinary tract_infection," *Wikipedia,* last modified March 29, 2015 en.wikipedia.org/wiki/Urinary_tract_infection.

2. Rossi R, Porta S, Canovi B. "Overview on cranberry and urinary tract infections in females," *J Clin Gastroenterology* 44 Suppl 1 (2010 Sep): S61-2. Review. PubMed PMID: 20495471. doi:10.1097/MCG.0b013e3181d2dc8e.

3. "Cranberry juice," *Wikipedia,* last modified February 4, 2015, *en.wikipedia.org/wiki/Cranberry_juice.*

4. Jepson RG, Williams G, Craig JC., "Cranberries for preventing urinary tract infections," *Cochrane Database Syst Rev.* 10 (2012 Oct 17): CD001321. Review. PubMed PMID: 23076891. doi:10.1002/14651858.CD001321.pub5.

5. Jepson R, Craig J, Williams G., "Cranberry products and prevention of urinary tract infections," *JAMA* 310, no. 13 (2013 Oct 2): 1395-6. PubMed PMID: 24084925. doi:10.1001/jama.2013.277509.

6. "Preventing UTIs," The Dr. Oz Television show, posted December 17, 2009, *http://www.doctoroz.com/videos/preventing-utis.*

IV. What is a fistula?

1. "Fistula," *Wikipedia*, last modified March, 15, 2015, http://en.wikipedia.org/wiki/Fistula.

2. Intestinal Complications accessed 07/31/2015, http://www.ccfa.org/resources/intestinal-complications.html

3. Arrowsmith SD, Ruminjo J, Landry EG. "Current practices in treatment of female genital fistula: a cross-sectional study," *BMC Pregnancy Childbirth* (2010 Nov 10) 10:73. PMID: 21067606; PubMed Central PMCID: PMC2995487. doi:10.1186/1471-2393-10-73.

4. Barone MA, Frajzyngier V, Arrowsmith S, Ruminjo J, Seuc A, Landry E, Beattie K, Barry TH, Lewis A, Muleta M, Nembunzu D, Olupot R, Sunday-Adeoye I, Wakasiaka WK, Widmer M, Gülmezoglu AM "Noninferiority of short-term urethral catheterization following fistula repair surgery: study protocol for a randomized controlled trial," *BMC Womens Health* 12 (2012 Mar 20): 5. PMID: 22433581; PubMed Central PMCID: PMC3353217 ClinicalTrials.gov Identifier: NCT01428830. doi:10.1186/1472-6874-12-5.

5. Wax, E. "A Brutal Legacy of Congo War" *Washington Post* Foreign Service. *The Washington Post*, (Saturday, October 25, 2003); Page A01.

6: Murray C, Goh JT, Fynes M, Carey MP. "Urinary and fecal incontinence following delayed primary repair of obstetric genital fistula," *BJOG* 109, no. 7 (2002 Jul): 828-32. PMID 12135221.

7. Browning A. "Risk factors for developing residual urinary incontinence after obstetric fistula repair," *Br J Obstet Gynaecol*, 113 (2006): 482-485.

V. Are stem cell therapies available for bladder disease?

1. Li Y, Wu WH, Hsu CW, Nguyen HV, Tsai YT, Chan L, Nagasaki T, Maumenee IH, Yannuzzi LA, Hoang QV, Hua H, Egli D, Tsang SH. "Gene therapy in patient-specific stem cell lines and a preclinical model of retinitis pigmentosa with membrane frizzled-related protein (MFRP) defects," *Mol Ther.* 22, no. 9 (2014 Sep): 1688-97. Patient-Specific Stem Cells and Personalized Gene Therapy: Patients' own cells transformed into model for studying disease and developing potential treatment, accessed February 27, 2015, http://newsroom.cumc.columbia.edu/blog/2014/07/10/stem-cells-personalized-gene-therapy/.

2. "Stem cell: Key Research Events in Stem Cell Research," *Wikipedia,* accessed March 1, 2015, http://en.wikipedia.org/wiki/Stem_cell#Key_research_events.

3. "Stem Cell Primer Basics," California Institute for Regenerative Medicine, accessed March 1, 2015, https://www.cirm.ca.gov/our-progress/stem-cell-basics.

4. "Safety of Blood Transfusions," accessed April 10, 2015, http://www.lls.org/content/nationalcontent/resourcecenter/freeeducationmaterials/treatments/pdf/bloodtransfusion.pdf

5. Kim, J. H., S.-R. Lee, Y. S. Song, H. J. Lee, "Stem Cell Therapy in Bladder Dysfunction: Where are we? And where do we have to go?," *BioMed Research International* (2013): 930713, Epub (2013 Sep 16), PMCID: PMC3787556 PMID: 24151627. doi:10.1155/2013/930713.

6. Nishijima, S., K. Sugaya, M. Miyazato, et al. "Restoration of bladder contraction by bone marrow transplantation in rats with underactive bladder," *Biomedical Research* 28, no. 5 (2007): 275-280.

7. Chen S., H.-Y. Zhang, N. Zhang, et al. "Treatment for chronic ischaemia-induced bladder detrusor dysfunction using bone marrow mesenchymal stem cells: an experimental study," *International Journal of Molecular Medicine* 29, no. 3 (2012): 416-422.

8. Huang, Y. C., A. W. Shindel, H. Ning, *et al.*, "Adipose derived stem cells ameliorate hyperlipidemia associated detrusor overactivity in a rat model," *Journal of Urology* 183, no. 3 (2010): 1232-1240.

9. Song, Y. S., H. J. Lee, Doo, S. H., et al., "Mesenchymal stem cells overexpressing hepatocyte growth factor (HGF) inhibit collagen deposit and improve bladder function in rat model of bladder outlet obstruction," *Cell Transplant* 21, no. 8 (2012): 1641-1650.

10. Hu, Y., L. M. Liao, Y. H. Ju, G. Fu, H. Y. Zhang, and H. X. Wu, "Intravenously transplanted bone marrow stromal cells promote recovery of lower urinary tract function in rats with complete spinal cord injury," *Spinal Cord* 50, no. 3 (2012): 202-207.

11. Nitta, M., T. Tamaki, K. Tono et al. "Reconstitution of experimental Neurogenic Bladder dysfunction using skeletal muscle-derived multipotent stem cells," *Transplantation* 89,, no. 9 (2010): 1043-1049.

12. Mitterberger, G. M., M. Pinggera, R. Marksteiner, *et al.*, "Adult stem cell therapy of female stress urinary incontinence," *European Urology* 53, no. 1 (2008): 169-175.

VI. How do you find valid, relevant medical information?

Research Tools:

"MedlinePlus: trusted health information for you," last modified April 8, 2015, http://www.nlm.nih.gov/medlineplus/medlineplus.html.

"Bookshelf: provides free online access to books and documents in life science and health care. Search, read, and discover," accessed April 8, 2015, http://www.ncbi.nlm.nih.gov/books.

1. Roza, Greg. *Inside the Human Body: Using Scientific and Exponential Notation*, The Rosen Publishing Group, (2007): 21.

2. Trudy Triumph Neurogenic Bladder and Bowel Blog, http://www.neurogenicbladder.com/.

3. Thoughts To Leave With You

1. Roza, Greg. *Inside the Human Body: Using Scientific and Exponential Notation*, The Rosen Publishing Group, (2007): 21.

2. Definition of Urinary Incontinence, http://ghr.nlm.nih.gov/glossary=urinary-incontinence/.

Index of Terms

Acknowledgments

—JoAnne Lake, Author

When I imagine the reaction of my friends and family to this book and its topic, I feel a bit queasy because, after reading this, they will have had a peek into my very private life. Part of me does not exactly want to be remembered in connection with a toilet, yet I see toileting dysfunction as a last frontier of topics that need to have mature acceptance and an active audience. So, I plow ahead, in spite of the hazards, to reassure others afflicted with bladder and bowel disorders that they are not alone, that there are ways to cope, and life can be wonderfully lived.

First of all, I would like to thank my compassionate, brilliant, and encouraging husband, Randy Lake. He is my partner in life, and I am so very grateful. He has been on this journey with me and has shared every part of it with me 100 percent. He has been supportive of my wrestling with issues as a patient, writing the blog TrudyTriumph.com, and then putting together this book. The topic opens up aspects of our private life as well. He agrees with me that this story will help people, so he is willing to lay his privacy aside.

I wish to thank Louise Sargent, who led a writing class I attended several evenings after work following my initial diagnosis. I was feeling the need to journal but did not have the confidence to go further. The class opened the floodgates for me. I thank her for that. She inspired me to write and gave me practical advice.

When I started on the venture, I discovered I would need to consult with many others, especially since I had never before embarked on such an adventure. After writing a hefty amount, I went on the hunt to find an editor. But how does one find such a person? While at my urologist's office, I wrote down every editor connected to the urology journals I saw in the waiting room. I started making calls. In the end, that was a good place to start.

I simply got lucky. I connected with a real person who took the time to talk to me. When I explained that I had an idea for a book and had about a one-hundred-page manuscript, she was interested. Her heart was heavy because her husband had just been diagnosed with a Neurogenic Bladder. She had empathy for me and was encouraging when I told her my ideas. She could not help me directly, but she told me she could refer me to a really nice editor who might be willing to help. So I called Lauren Baker, the nice editor, who told me to e-mail what I had to her. A few days later, she got back to me. She did not laugh at my very disorganized and simple first attempt, but kindly sent me on to Mary Colleen Jenkins, another editor and writing coach. Mary Colleen took my secrets and ideas in hand and helped me organize the stew of thoughts that have become this book. This book started out as just a dream, but in the end, many people believed in its value and helped me see it through. I am so very grateful for their support and confidence.

My luck did not end there. I have a dear friend, Julia Parker, who is a research medical librarian who really believed in this dream and made it her dream, too. When Julia started adding her research and grounded ideas, we got excited because the manuscript became balanced, complete, and credible, my story and her in-depth research, like yin and yang.

Along the way, I had proofreaders who provided me sound advice: Susan Kopczynski Jostrom, Kathy Imahara, Susan Engle, Joan Burt, Elaine Plummer, Mary Etter, Sandy Newcomb, and Renee Meade. They gave me great ideas and confidence to continue. I also want to thank the people, some anonymous and some not, who have shared their heartfelt stories and expertise with us. Scott Beckert RN, with years of experience in the field of incontinence, freely gave his time and expertise in helping me understand the types of products that are available to persons with Neurogenic Bladder and Bowel.

I had an encouraging writing coach, the kind and so-very-talented editor Becky Fish. She helped the story fit together and make it ready for you to read. Lastly, I want to thank Cathy Bromley, our copy editor.

—JoAnne Lake, aka "Trudy Triumph"

JoAnne lives in the Seattle area with her husband Randy and dog Rainey. She is the mother of four grown children and wonderful grandchildren. JoAnne's wisdom is the result of challenges met head-on and experiences as a patient, wife, mother, educator, and friend. She graduated with a BA from Washington State University and a fifth year from Seattle University.

Journaling her private thoughts and feelings, she started writing an anonymous blog in 2012. This is her first book.

Visit JoAnne Lake (as Trudy Triumph) at her website www.TrudyTriumph.com.

Julia Parker is known as the "Biosleuth." She is a researcher of patent, scientific, medical, and company information by education and training. She has worked in nonprofit and biopharmaceutical research and developmental sectors, as well as in clinical, academic, and public settings.

Julia holds a BS in Microbiology from Purdue University, an MS in Pathobiology – SPHCM from the University of Washington, and an MLIS from the University of Washington.

JoAnne's story is researched and validated by her.